And they shall be called the Sons of GOD

Hell is coming to the World and the Church is responsible for it

Tolulope Oyewole
Foreword by Debbie Shobo-Oyewole

Published by TAOO Publishing

Scripture quotations are taken from various translation of the Bible as indicated on the pages. All copyrights acknowledged.

© June 2018, TAOO Publishing. All rights reserved.

This book is subject to conditions that it shall not by way of trade or otherwise, be lent, resold, hired, reproduced in whole or in part in any form or otherwise circulated without the author's prior consent in any form of binding or cover other than that which it is published and without similar conditions being imposed on the subsequent purchaser.

All rights reserved under international copyright law.

All rights reserved, this book or any part thereof, may not be produced, stored in or introduced into a retrieval system, or transmitted, in any form or by any means electronic, mechanical, photocopy, recording or otherwise without the written permission of the publisher.

PUBLISHED BY TAOO PUBLISHING

Dedication

To Michael Oluwatileyin Shosanya, a vibrant young man who went home too soon. Though you may be lost to us, we know you are found in Christ.

To my lovely wife – Debbie Shobo-Oyewole, who has always been a source of comfort and joy to me and everyone around us. I am glad to spend forever with you under the Lordship of our Lord Jesus Christ.

To my lady, the bride of my Lord, to whom I am called to be a Prophet and an Evangelist in this generation.

Content

	Appreciation	5
	Foreword	7
Preface:	I hear the Sound of the Abundance of Rain	9
Chapter 1:	The Habitations of Cruelty	11
Chapter 2:	The Groanings and Expectation of Creation	19
Chapter 3:	God is Judging in the Council of gods	25
Chapter 4:	Ignorance, the Identity Killer, and Thief	30
Chapter 5:	The Spirit and the Church	43
Chapter 6:	The Children and Heirs	53
Chapter 7:	The Manifestation of the Sons of God	58
Chapter 8:	Stand Up and Take Charge	75
Chapter 9:	Rewards and Judgment	81
Chapter 10:	The Principle of the Chosen	85
Epilogue:	A Message to the Church	93

Appreciation

I am grateful to God my Father, for gracing me with this message to bring to His Church at this time. It is my prayer that I have done as instructed and not missed His will at any point in the journey of producing this message. And if I have, I pray that His truth will eclipse our hearts.

I am grateful for the love and support and contribution of my wonderful wife, Debbie Shobo-Oyewole. She has indeed been a rock and a source of encouragement to me. I look forward to forever with you.

I am grateful for my Youth Pastor and mentor, Pastor Damilola Ogunlade for his continuous encouragement and for taking the time to challenge me on some of the truth presented in this book. It is a privilege to be serving under him.

I am grateful for the support and contributions of my mentee, Oluwaseun Samuel Iyikanmi (the Timothy to my Paul), my true son. I am grateful to God for the man of God that he is growing up to be.

I am grateful to my proof-readers, my namesake Tolulope Ojo-Williams and Anna Kumi – both of whom are very dear sisters to me.

I will like to acknowledge my local Church – the New Covenant Cherubim and Seraphim Church, especially the Youth of Covenant where I serve as a part of the leadership team. These men and women of God I serve with are truly inspirational; they are indeed the best team I have ever been privileged to work with.

I am grateful for my SAGE (Saving a Generation Endangered)

family and friends. You all have been a source of joy to me. I am especially grateful to Tobi Olujimi, who serves as our leader and Pastor Adebayo-Oke (aka Chief), who serves as our Pastor and father.

Last but not the least; I am grateful for my family – both the Oyewole and Shobo families, for your constant support and prayers. **I love you all!**

Foreword

As the Wife, friend, companion and Helper of Tolulope Oyewole, I could not help but be swept by the idea of *"And they shall be called the Sons of God."* This concept had been an inspiration that the Holy Spirit laid on his heart for a while now and having both worked in the Youth Ministry for some years now, we have noticed a clear need for practical discipleship for the growing Christian. This statement is not a judgment placed on a particular body, but a wakeup call for the entire Christian body.

The '......*Sons of God*' was a notion I initially defined as just children or heirs of God. However, this book helped to illustrate a deeper meaning of what it means to be a son of God. The book starts with the explanation of the beginning of time and the creation of the world. The beginning of time as we know it has been precisely broken down and explained to further our understanding. **ROMANS 8: 14** *"For as many as are led by the Spirit of God, these are sons of God."* Therefore, being created by God is not enough to be a Son of God, but we are qualified by following the lead of the Holy Spirit. In the same way, we become the Sons of whatever we are led by. What are you led by?

I have noticed the sudden rise of leaders and prophets that claim to be ambassadors for Christ. Many unfortunately have been led astray by the false ones. Tolu reminds us to be aware of the spiritual forces that have been put in place against God's people. Ephesians 6:12 *"For we do not wrestle against flesh and blood, but against power, against rulers of the darkness of this age, against spiritual hosts of wickedness in the heavenly places."* They are many things against us as Sons of God. As **PSALM 1** illustrates, we must be careful to walk with the Godly, and not to stand in the way of sinners. God has promised to bless those who meditate on His words day and night. You shall not wither, but everything you do, you shall prosper.

Though we have not seen God, we have seen Him in His works, we have seen the power of His hands. Our hearts testify of the goodness of God. For this reason, I advise you to read beyond the words you see. Ponder on the instructions of the Holy Spirit and the position in which He has placed you. I am always reminded that though I am not where I want to be, praise the Lord, I am not where I used to be. I cannot do enough justice to what I know this book will do for the kingdom of God. Let us open our eyes; our life is not ours, we must submit it to God. God is interested in the image in which He has made us, and not the perverted image the world has portrayed. It is time for us to put back on the image God has made us in unless we will experience His wrath, just as the sons of disobedience did.

I am moved, and I am passionate for Christ, for God has done an amazing thing in my husband's life and continued to do so. Life has not promised a bed of roses, but we rest assured that God loves us and keeps us secure. This book has awakened my mind and has encouraged me to broaden my perception of the scriptures. I encourage you to read it on a good ground (your heart) and prepare it to receive the truth. I also urge you, to pass on what you've have learnt as it pleases God for His truth and gospel to reach the nations and generations to come. My prayer for this nation and you is that we will know God, to love Him and to glorify Him. **God will do something new. The time is now! Take your position, hold your mantle and be led by God as Sons of God.**

Debbie Shobo-Oyewole

Preface
I hear the Sound of Abundance of Rain

The message that God has graced me to present in this book has been burning in my heart for many years now. I have often wondered what the best way would be to begin the message, but one thing I know for sure is that this message could not have come at a better time:

> **Because, this year, we will see the manifestation of the Holy Spirit like never before and it will mark the beginning of the greatest revival in Christian history.**

I say this for two reasons:

Since the middle of last year - 2017, God had been speaking to me about the manifestation of His Spirit this year. Initially, I thought this message was just for young people, but now, I am inclined to believe that this will cut across the entire Church.

The second reason is, many years ago, a prophecy was given that when Oral Roberts and Billie Graham go to be with the Lord, the greatest revival in Christian history will begin. Early this year, we said farewell to the great revivalist in modern history – Billie Graham, Oral Roberts - having passed away a few years before him. I heard about this prophesy when Pastor Benny Hinn – Tele-Evangelist spoke about it on Trinity Broadcasting Network about five years ago, and he also did an interview about it early this year, just after the death of Billie Graham.

Now that these veterans of the Lord's army are with Him, the criteria for the prophecy have been met. Therefore, I hear the sound of abundance of rain. The question for the Church now is:

are our cisterns ready to receive the abundance?

It's so sad, however, that at the time when we are about to experience a new outpouring of the Holy Spirit, we are also witnessing the death of young people like never before. In London, about 50 young people have either been stabbed or shot from January to April this year. The Lord warned me about this a decade ago in a revelation:

> **"Under the inspiration of the Holy Spirit, I was given a revelation in a dream. In the dream, I entered a particular room, and I saw youths sitting around and in front of them was another group of dead looking youths, some of which had gun wounds, and some had knife wounds. These dead looking youths began to speak; they said that more youths would die as they take their focus away from God. They also said these killings would get worse and churches will also be badly affected – even burnt down!"**

The recent happenings in the City of London, as well as the revelation, are wake-up calls to the Church, one that we cannot afford to ignore or approach passively.

Therefore, the focus of this book is to call the sons of God to attention. By sons of God, I do not mean a gender position, but a place of authority. It is time for the sons of God to take their place and redeem the desolate heritages that have been the habitations of cruelty for so long (**PSALM 74:20**) ...

Chapter 1
The Habitations of Cruelty

There have been legends of the Greek, Roman, Yoruba and Scandinavian Pantheons. Zeus is the head of the Greek Pantheon, Jupiter the head of the Roman Pantheon, Oludumare as the head of the Yoruba Pantheon and Odin as the head of the Scandinavian Pantheon (all these chief gods are also referred to as "*god of the sky or the heavens*"). While history sometimes presents them as folktales, there are some indications of their existence in scripture, which in some measure matches up with their legend.

In **GENESIS 6:2**, we are presented with a semblance of these creatures. They were called the sons of God, or you may also call them the sons of Heaven. The scripture informs us that these creatures lusted after the daughters of men and took them as wives. The offspring they produced grew to become the mighty men of the Earth. Although further information was not provided, their description is tangential to the demi-gods of folklore. However, we see that the interaction of the sons of God with daughters of men led to God condemning the human race and entire world with them to destruction by flood.

God's judgment on the world as a result of the interference of these sons of God shows that their purpose was at odds with Him. The question here, therefore, is: how can God's sons be at odds with Him? Are they then, indeed, sons of God? The word "*sons*" is translated from the Hebrew word "*ben*," which means "*builder of the family name.*" This word does not necessarily mean a direct offspring but can also mean someone that carries the presence of another or a representative of someone. Angels fall into the category of representatives of God because they serve as His messengers. The next appearance of these creatures gives us a clearer picture of who they are.

In **Job 1:6**, the Bible informs that these sons of God presented themselves to the LORD. Amongst them was Satan, who God cast out from Heaven because he longed to take the place of God. This was depicted in **Revelations 12: 7 – 9**, we see that he was cast out with his angels. So, he was not alone. These are known as the fallen angels, and they have set themselves at odds with the LORD, to undermine His creation – with humanity being the primary target (**Revelations 12:17**). This resolution continues today.

Let's Get Some Context

To give some context to the notion of the sons of God being the fallen angels, of which Lucifer (Satan) is Chief amongst them, let's review the creation account:

"In the beginning God created the heavens and the earth. The earth was without form, and void; and darkness was on the face of the deep. And the Spirit of God was hovering over the face of the waters" (**Genesis 1: 1 – 2 NKJV**).

Before time began, God created the heavens and the Earth as portrayed in Genesis 1:1. However, the following verse shows us that the Earth was without form, and darkness covered the face of the deep. Some scholars believe that this was not the original form of the Earth at the point of creation. The idea behind this is that if the heavens were not without form when they were created, why was the Earth? It is, therefore, believed that something happened between **Genesis 1:1** and **1:2** to change the state of the Earth. This concept is called the gap theory.

To determine the possibility of the gap theory being true, let us examine the following:

- **"Without form,"** from the Hebrew word **"tahu,"** which synonymises desolation, waste, wilderness, confusion.

- **"Void,"** from the Hebrew word **"bohu,"** which synonymises emptiness and ruin.

- **"Darkness,"** from the Hebrew word **"choshek,"** which synonymises misery, death, destruction, sorrow, ignorance, and obscurity.

Given the above, GENESIS 1:2 can read:

- "The Earth was desolate and empty, and death was over the face of the deep."

- "The Earth was a wasteland and in ruin and there was destruction over the face of the deep."

- "The Earth was in confusion and ruin; misery, sorrow, and ignorance covered the face of the deep."

Putting the three together will read:

"The Earth was a desolate wasteland, full of confusion and it was in complete ruin. Misery, sorrow and ignorance covered the surface of the deep, leading to death and destruction."

The rephrasing of the passage as presented above gives a different perspective and picture from what was imprinted in our minds at Sunday school. They show that the Earth became destroyed at some point, instead of it initially being created that way.

We know from **REVELATIONS 12**, **ISAIAH 14** and **EZEKIEL 28** that Satan was cast out to the Earth, indicating that his presence and that of his angels brought destruction to the Earth. Therefore, the Earth became the habitation of darkness and cruelty – a desolate heritage.

The statement that comes after – in the same verse - further proves this notion. It says that the Holy Spirit moved off the face of the deep. To understand what this means, let's consider the implication of the word **"move."** The Hebrew word used for **"move"** was **"rachaph,"** which synonymises flutter (to fly unsteadily) and shake (to tremble). Based on the synonyms mentioned above, the statement can be thus read as:

- "The Holy Spirit flew unsteadily over the surface of the deep."

- "The Holy Spirit shook the surface of the deep."

Putting them together will read:

"The Holy Spirit flew unsteadily over the surface of the deep and caused them to tremble."

The above rendering implies that the Holy Spirit went out to war against the forces of darkness living on the Earth – the fallen angels, to bring the Earth back under the domain of God. Therefore, what we know as the creation of the Earth was the redeeming and restoration of what previously existed.

The Link between Fallen Angels and the Ancient Pantheons

There are two main links between fallen angels and the ancient Pantheons:

1. Mythology showed that they mostly ruled humans with cruelty and sometimes human sacrifices were made to them

2. Mythology also showed that they procreated with the daughters of men

The first link shows that these ancient gods had a similar nature to the fallen angels and like Lucifer, they craved to be worship by humans and to hold them in bondage.

The second link is more direct as it correlates with what the Bible says about the fallen angels.

Paul, in his letter to the Church at Ephesus further revealed the identity of these beings and their ranking in the kingdom of darkness:

***"For we do not wrestle against flesh and blood, but against principalities, against powers, against the rulers of the darkness of this age, against spiritual hosts of wickedness in the heavenly places."* (EPHESIANS 6:12 NKJV)**

In this verse of scripture, Paul identifies the following classes of spiritual beings:

- Principalities

- Powers

- Rulers of the darkness of this age

- Spiritual hosts of wickedness in heavenly places

It is my opinion, from studying the Bible that these are classes of angels. We have the Cherubs, Seraph, Archangels and so on. In the book of **EZEKIEL**, we see manifestations of some of these different types of angels, so also in the books of **ISAIAH** and **REVELATIONS**. In the book of **REVELATIONS**, John described the Angels who stood at the four corners of the Earth: one holding the four winds of the Earth; another angel arising from the east with the seal of God in his hands, giving orders to the four angels not to harm anyone on the Earth; and another mighty angel who stood on the seas and land and swore by the Lord (REVELATIONS 7: 1 – 3; 10: 1 – 6). Also, when Gabriel appeared to Zacharias, he told him that he always stands in the presence of God (LUKE 1:19). Thus, signifying that not every angel stands in the presence of God. Jesus confirmed this statement when He said the angels of children always see the face of God (MATTHEW 10:18).

These scriptures show that there is an angelic hierarchy in Heaven and some angels have command over other angels, just as Lucifer did when he was in Heaven. Therefore, we can assume that there is also a hierarchy in the kingdom of darkness and if we consider the information provided to us by Paul, the hierarchical order will look like this:

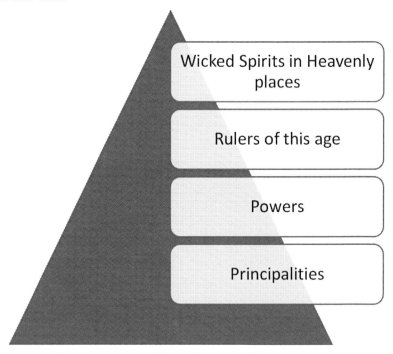

From my understanding of the Bible and the revelation given to me by God, this is what I can deduce about these beings:

- **Principalities** – angelic beings placed over nations, which include geographical countries, professions, families, religions and even particular Christian denomination.

- **Powers** – angelic beings that have control over the elements of this world, such as water, iron, air, diseases and so on. Though these are similar to the pantheons in folklore, however, I decided not to include them in this category, because folklore regards them as the highest spiritual beings.

- **Rulers of this age** – these are angelic beings who have been given season to bring disaster on the Earth – usually on a global scale and control the affairs of the Earth for a particular season. Examples of these are the Anti-Christ, false prophet and the four horsemen of the apocalypse.

- **Spiritual wickedness in heavenly places** – these are the most superior angelic beings in the kingdom of darkness, and the chief amongst them is Satan. These beings operate from the heavens and control the operation of the other three beings. They are the ones described by Jude as dignitaries **(JUDE 1: 8 – 10)**, and Peter confirmed this statement in his second letter to the Church **(2 PETER 2:11)**. I believe that these represent the Pantheons in mythology and all their chief gods are a prototype of Satan. Think about it, who else will want to claim to have created and given life to humans if not him?

Why is all this important?

It is essential to establish the possibilities of what happened eons ago so that the Church understands the significance of her role on the Earth. After God had restored the Earth, He willed it to Adam and made Him god over the Earth. God's purpose for Adam was to rule the Earth and manage God's creation. However, when Satan deceived Adam, the Earth was brought back to his domain, because one of the eternal laws that govern creation is that we are slaves to who or what we listen to. Therefore, Adam became a slave of Satan when he listened to him above God, giving Satan authority over everything Adam had. Therefore, the reign of the four class of Satanic angels (mentioned above) was reinstated, and the Earth is reverting to a state of desolation and chaos, just as it was in **GENESIS 1:2**.

If we look at the world today, you will see that it bears a striking resemblance to what was described in the first part of **GENESIS 1:2**. It is fast becoming a wasteland, void of love and full of confusion, sorrow, and misery, resulting in death and destruction. All because most of humanity is under the influence of Satan and except the true sons of God – the Church, arise and take their place, the Earth will be utterly destroyed, just as it was eons ago.

Chapter 2
The Groanings and Expectation of Creation

Many years ago, the Lord told me that the reason why Satan has a lot of influence on the Earth is because humanity at large is still under his control, even the Church. Though the Church was established by Christ as a continuation of His existence on Earth - after His death, resurrection, and ascension ass His representation on the Earth. However, we too have sadly been infiltrated by Satan, because instead of us standing out as the light – we have decided to blend in with the darkness.

The Death and Destruction of the World

The threat of global warming, the killings of young people, economic turmoil, terrorism (including mass shootings), religious conflict, ethnic cleansing, gentrification, gender neutrality, homosexuality, gross immorality at leadership, the corruption of the Youth and children, the war in Syria and the threat of war all over the world. These are all signs that the world is fast returning to the chaos and formlessness it was in **GENESIS 1:2**. The world is dying. It is under a curse! The entirety of creation is groaning and crying out for their redemption from the scepter of cruelty, but this can only happen when the sons of God take their place.

The Theory of Nations

Every nation is under the influence of a principality. Principalities are angelic beings; they are either God's angels or Satan's. The type of Principality assigned to a nation is determined by what the majority of that nation is focused on. If a nation is focused on pleasing God, the Principality set over that nation will be from God, and if they concentrate on self-indulgence and carnal endeavours, the Principality would be from Satan.

Please note that a nation does not have to be geographical. The word **"nation"** comes from the Greek word *"ethnos"* which refers to a group of people who share the same heritage, belief, culture, and language. Therefore, a nation can be a family, a professional group, a social club, a denomination, or a country. Whatever the magnitude of this nation, they are all under the influence of a Principality.

The book of **DANIEL** gives a clear picture of this reality. After Daniel had fasted for twenty-one days, the Angel Gabriel appeared to him to provide him with the message God had sent to him. In this encounter, it was revealed to Daniel that the message was sent the exact day he set his heart to understand, but the Principality of Persia stopped the Angel from delivering this message. Now take note that the Angel qualified the being as the Principality of Persia, the kingdom that influenced the region Daniel was living in. This Principality was undoubtedly a Satanic one because it stood to resist the angel of God from bringing God's message to His people. Therefore, this shows that the people of Persia did not belong to God and it was the role of this being to prevent the will of God to take place in all the regions under the rule of Persia and to keep them in bondage.

The Angel Gabriel then went on to tell Daniel that the Prince of Greece will soon come. He later revealed to him about a wild goat with one horn who attacked an animal with two horns and destroyed it. What the angel told him was a foretelling of how Alexander the Great would invade Babylon and destroy the power of Medes and Persia. This occurrence happened a few years after the revelation was given to Daniel. Please note that before Gabriel told Daniel about Alexander, he mentioned the coming of the

Prince of Greece. Therefore, this indicates that the Principalities over regions work directly with their leaders and before any battle is won in the physical, it has first been fought and won in the realm of the spirit. Thus, the writer of the epistle to Hebrews states:

"By faith we understand that the worlds were framed by the word of God, so that the things which are seen were not made of things which are visible" **(HEBREWS 11:3 NKJV)**.

Principalities also make specific requirements from people under their influence. We see examples of this throughout scripture and history:

1. The Principality over the region of Moab, called Baal of Peor required prostitution as a sacrifice to it. The children of Israel encountered the influence of this principality when they passed through the region of Moab in **NUMBERS 25**.

2. Over a Canaanite region, the principality called Molech required child sacrifices by fire (**LEVITICUS 18:21**). This custom was one of the reasons why God was ejecting the Canaanites out of their land and bringing the children of Israel in their place. Through this, God was redeeming the land from the bondage of Molech.

3. In the Eastern part of Nigeria, an Igbo deity called Amadioha required that twins be sacrificed to it until Mary Slessor – a Scottish Christian missionary to Nigeria led the abolishing of these sacrifices.

Though these acts on the surface may seem like superstitious acts of a backward community, they were more than that; they were, in fact, demonic inspirations.

The Access Point

Many people blame God for the catastrophes on the Earth. A famous atheist once said that God is not great and in fact, the world will be a better place without Him. One thing we fail to realise is that God has willed the Earth to humanity (**PSALM 115:16**). Therefore, we are responsible for everything that happens here. From the time Satan deceived Adam, humanity has handed over the authority of the Earth to him. Having said this, however, we still hold the title deed to the Earth – it is still our possession, but if we are not conscious of this, we will be destroyed with the Earth.

The Lord told me that no spiritual being has access to the Earth except through the agency of man. Therefore, God or Satan cannot do anything on the Earth except through the participation of a human being. This is why God raised prophets and Judges to deliver his people whenever they turned away from Him. In the same way, Satan inspires people to sin against God whenever he wants to bring destruction.

A case in point is David. When God wanted to deliver the people of Israel entirely from the might of the Philistines, He sent Samuel to anoint David as king. The Bible states from that moment on, the Spirit of God began to move David and even brought him into the palace to learn how to run the affairs of the palace as a steward of the current king, Saul. David ministered to him through music to soothe him whenever he was being tortured by the demons God allowed to torment him. Saul loved David very much, and so did Jonathan, his son, and heir apparent.

One day, the Spirit of God orchestrated for David to be present when Goliath defiled the armies of Israel through taunting and cursing; calling out the champion of Israel to face him in a deciding battle. He taunted them for forty days, until David showed up and, through the inspiration of Holy Spirit, defeated Goliath, thus putting the Philistine army to flight.

After this incident, Saul became jealous of David, and whenever the evil spirit possessed him, rather than being soothed by David's music, he would try to kill him. On at least two occasions, Saul, under the influence of demons, tried to pin David to the wall with a spear. Here we see that Satan tried to stop the rise of a great king that God has chosen for Himself to deliver His people and cause them to possess their full inheritance. This was achieved during the reign of David (however, Satan wanting to stop this, influenced Saul to commit the remainder his reign in hot pursuit of David to kill him.) The influence of Satan was so strong over Saul that he even wiped out an entire town of priests, saving only one - who escaped by the skin of his teeth.

Fast forward to when David became king. One day he had an idea to hold a census, forgetting that God said whenever a census is carried out, every soul that is counted has to be redeemed. When the story was told in **FIRST CHRONICLES CHAPTER 21 VERSE 1**, we saw the hidden figure behind the census. The Bible states that Satan stood against the nation of Israel and caused or inspired David to hold a census. So, Satan was looking for a cause to accuse the nation of Israel before God and thus caused them to sin by misleading David.

This example is akin to when Herod was inspired to kill all the children within the age range of zero to two years old, in the exertion to kill Jesus Christ and rob humanity of our Saviour. However, this was averted when God appeared to Joseph in a dream and told him to take Jesus to Egypt (**MATTHEW 2: 16 – 21**).

The above examples show that from the time humanity was given the reins of the Earth; Satan has been working to influence us to destroy the creation of God. The question, therefore, is how does he do this? What the Lord told me is that the thoughts of man are the portal by which God or Satan influences the world. Therefore, this means that every act of evil, wickedness, destruction, nobility, honesty, and goodness is inspired by a thought. Thoughts inspire every action we take, and our thoughts either come from God or Satan. Whoever we obey, is the one to whom we become enslaved. The activities of Satan first start with a thought which, once obeyed, produces an action, then leads to a habit or mindset, then it becomes an obsession, leading to possession until we get to the place of consumption and destruction.

If we study modern history, you can see the trail the enemy has left. From slavery to imperialism, racism, the rise of communism, the Jewish holocaust, the world wars, white supremacy, black on black violence, sexual pervasion, gender-neutral lifestyle, killings and others. All these are thoughts that the enemy has used to derail the human race. The more we obey him, the stronger his influence on us and more so, the stronger his influence on the world.

The cruelty and disasters we see today are as a direct result of this influence. Even what we call acts of God, are sometimes devoid of God's involvement. Do not get me wrong. I do think that God sends disaster on the Earth as judgment for the wickedness of the world and also as a way of protecting those who put their trust in Him. However, a majority of these so-called acts of God are symptoms of the Earth's destruction as a result of the curse that came upon creation – just like a fever can be a symptom of an infection. Other times, however, I believe it is Satan exercising his influence on the Earth as a result of enslaving a significant proportion of the human race. Satan's influence will continue to bring destruction to the human race if the sons of God do not rise and take their place.

Chapter 3
God is Judging in the Council of gods

In chapter 1, I referred to several Pantheons that we have come across in history – from the Greek Pantheon to the Roman Pantheon, the Yoruba Pantheon and the Scandinavian Pantheons. However, there is a Pantheon that supersedes all Pantheons, and that is the Christian Pantheon.

PSALM 82, presents this Pantheon to us:

*"God stands in the congregation of the mighty; He judges among the gods. How long will you judge unjustly, and show partiality to the wicked? Selah." (**PSALM 82:1 NKJV**)*

This scripture poses two questions: who are these gods and how is it possible for there to be other gods apart from the one true God?

To answer these questions, let us consider **VERSES 6** and **7**:

I said, "You are gods, and all of you are children of the Most High. But you shall die like men, and fall like one of the princes." **NKJV**

Three things are striking in this passage:

God said they are gods

1. They are called the children of the Most High

2. They are subject to death

I will be addressing the first two points in this chapter and the third in the next chapter.

God said they are gods

We know from the Genesis 1 and confirmed by Hebrews 11:3 that the creation of the world came by the utterance of God's word. Therefore, whatever God says, is. Since this is the case, we can conclude that these beings have the status of gods because God said so. This proclamation is of itself a legal tender that validates their identity, and in fact, this was the same proclamation Jesus quoted when the Jews accused Him of being blasphemous because He claimed an equal status with God (John 10:34).

The word **"gods"** is **"*Elohim*,"** this is the same Hebrew word used when referring to God as the creator. The word means – Supreme, Magistrate. These synonyms demonstrate that when God proclaimed Adam to have dominion over the Earth, what He was in fact saying was for him to be the god of the Earth. Therefore, God was in effect saying to Adam, *"I have said you are a god."* So, since God made that declaration to Adam at the beginning (knowing that God does not change His mind), it must mean that this declaration remains true for the human race.

They are called the children of the Most High

These beings are also called children of God. Therefore, this means that they share in nature of God. So, what makes them children of God?

JOHN 1: 12 – 13 presents us with the answer to this question:

But as many as received Him, to them He gave the right to become children of God, to those who believe in His name: who were born, not of blood, nor of the will of the flesh, nor of the will of man, but of God. **(NKJV)**

This scripture shows that we who believe in the person of Jesus Christ have the right to become the sons of God. Just as the law or constitution of a country provides the pathway to becoming a citizen of the country, also, the Bible – which is the constitution that governs all issues of life, has provided us with a pathway to becoming children of God and that is to believe in Jesus.

If we read **PSALM 82:6** in the context of **JOHN 1: 12 – 13**, we see that God was not addressing every human being. It is only addressing those who believe in Jesus. Therefore, the scripture was only addressing the Church.

Associates of the God-kind

Reading the verse 6 in the context of **VERSES 1** to **7** of **PSALM 86**, shows that the counsel of gods in which God stands to judge is the Church. Another scripture that gives a clear understanding of this is **2 PETER 1: 3 – 4**:

As His divine power has given to us all things that pertain to life and godliness, through the knowledge of Him who called us by glory and virtue, by which have been given to us exceedingly great and precious promises, that through these you may be partakers of the divine nature, having escaped the corruption that is in the world through lust (NKV).

The critical statement here that will help us understand the Church's connection to divinity or ascription of the status of gods is *"through these you may be partakers of the divine nature."* To better understand this phrase, lets us highlight the keywords and what they mean in the original Greek text:

1. "Partakers" – "*koinonos*," which means associates

2. "Divine" – "*Theios*," this is the Greek word for God

3. "Nature" – "*phusis*," which means type or kind

The phrase can now read: **"through these, you may be associates of the God-kind."**

The implication of this representation, based on the original Greek translation, shows that when we believe in Jesus – through Whom we have been called by glory and virtue - we become associates of the God-kind, partakers of the nature of God. Therefore, believing in Jesus makes us a new class of creatures. The following scriptures further support and explain this statement:

Therefore, if anyone is in Christ, he is a new creation; old things have passed away; behold, all things have become new. (2 CORINTHIANS 5:17 NKJV)

And so, it is written, "The first man Adam became a living being." The last Adam became a life-giving spirit. However, the spiritual is not first, but the natural, and afterward the spiritual. The first man was of the earth, made of dust; the second Man is the Lord from heaven. As was the man of dust, so also are those who are made of dust; and as is the heavenly Man, so also are those who are heavenly. And as we have borne the image of the man of dust, we shall also bear the image of the heavenly Man. (1 CORINTHIANS 15: 45 – 49 NKJV)

Both of these scriptures point to the creation of a new creature – note that **2 CORINTHIANS 5:17** did not say a new human being, but an entirely new creature. This creature is wholly disenfranchised from the first man – Adam, which **1 CORINTHIANS 15:45** described as the man of the Earth. But we who have believed are now after the second Adam, Jesus – Who the Bible describes as the man of Heaven. Therefore, we are no longer just humans, we are now gods, in the same way, Jesus is God.

Though this statement may seem controversial or even heretic or blasphemous, the following scriptures show that we share in the exact nature of Jesus Christ:

The Spirit Himself bears witness with our spirit that we are children of God, and if children, then heirs—heirs of God and joint heirs with Christ, if indeed we suffer with **Him,** *that we may also be glorified together.* (**Romans** 8: 16 – 17 NKJV)

Beloved, now we are children of God; and it has not yet been revealed what we shall be, but we know that when He is revealed, we shall be like Him, for we shall see Him as He is. (1 **John** 3:2 NKJV)

Love has been perfected among us in this: that we may have boldness in the day of judgment; because as He is, so are we in this world. (1 **John** 4:17)

These scriptures show beyond reasonable doubt that we who are in Christ Jesus are gods, we are the counsel of the mighty described in **Psalm 82:1** and we share in the same nature as Jesus. Therefore, as He is, so we are on the Earth – hence the proclamation of *"I have said you are gods."* However, the question is, why are we not manifesting our nature on the Earth as we are supposed to?

Chapter 4
Ignorance: The Identity Killer, and Thief

The third point to highlight in **Psalms 82: 7** is that though we are gods and share in the exact nature of Jesus Christ – we are subject to death:

"But you shall die like men, and fall like one of the princes." **(NKJV)**

The statement is paradoxical and very contradictory because we understand from the Bible that the second Adam – from Whom the Church comes from – is a life-giving Spirit. Therefore, death is contrary to our nature.

Another reason why this statement is contradictory is that death is a function of Satan. **John 10:9** tells us that Satan comes to kill, steal and destroy. Therefore, this means that though the Church is a pantheon of gods, we are still being influenced by the power of Satan.

So, why is this the case?

Hosea 4:6 states:

"My people are destroyed for lack of knowledge. Because you have rejected knowledge..." **(NKJV)**

2 Peter 1: 3 also states:

"As His divine power has given to us all things that pertain to life and godliness, through the knowledge of Him who called us by glory and virtue." **(NKJV)**

Both scriptures show that knowledge is a prerequisite to us walking in the divine nature and ignorance, robs us of it; producing death.

What you do not know kills you

This scripture shows that ignorance produces death and destruction. Imagine if you are dehydrated and on the brink of losing consciousness. If you do not know that drinking water can help revive you, chances are you will die of dehydration even though you are surrounded by drinking water.

Therefore, ignorance is a killer, and it is the reason why the Church has been subject to death – which manifests as dissension, division, sedition and other works of the flesh; to the point that the Church is now suffering the same fate as the world. For example, the divorce rate in the Church is the same as the world. The level of corruption in the Church is similar to the world. All this is happening because we do not know our identity and position on the Earth.

Ignorance is a thief

Ignorance robs you of what you have because if you do not know what you have, it becomes of no value to you or those around you – so you may as well not have it. Imagine if someone was willed an estate worth millions of pounds and they did not know it; will they enjoy the benefits of being a millionaire? Imagine if you had enough food in your house to last a lifetime, but you are not aware of it, will you experience the peace of not worrying about the next meal? It is in the same vein that many are leading a life contrary to their identity and lose the benefits of who they are, because of their ignorance.

I remember a sermon I heard many years ago about the story of an eagle that was raised by a mother hen. The eagle only led the life it was nurtured to lead, thus robbing it of its true identity. The Church is like this eagle, though it had the power to soar the skies, it still experiences pseudo-flights like its chicken companions. In the same vein, we the Church have the power to change our world, but yet we allow ourselves to be enslaved by it.

Why does the Church lack knowledge?

According to the Online Etymology Dictionary, the word **"ignorance" is** from the Old French word *"ignorant,"* and from the Latin word *"ignorantem,"* translating as **"not knowing,"** or the present participle *"ignorare,"* also translating as, **"to be unacquainted; mistake, misunderstand; take no notice of, pay no attention to,".** The etymology of the word, **"ignorance,"** suggests that the cause is not a scarcity of information, but the fact that information has not be pursued or has been ignored. Therefore, I define ignorance as a passive approach to truth.

It is this passivity that has created the vacuum for misinformation and deception within the Church. From this have come disputes that have divided Churches and led to scores of denominations within the Body of Christ.

There are three key truths that the Church has ignored or passively pursued:

- The knowledge of the nature of God

- The knowledge of true Biblical Doctrine and Worship

- The knowledge of the Lordship and Partnership of the Holy Spirit

The Knowledge of the nature of God

One of the strategies of Satan, which he has successfully implemented from the beginning of time, is to cause humans to question the nature of God. He used this strategy in the Garden of Eden when he persuaded Eve to eat out of the forbidden tree; He convinced her that God was holding out on humanity by preventing us from eating from the tree. Thus, creating a false image of God.

Sadly, the Church is plagued with this same false image of God and denominations are created based on their perception of who God is and what His will for humanity is. It is no wonder that the first two commandments God gave to the children of Israel – a prototype of the Church – addressed the issue of the false presentation of God. God was not just dealing with worshipping other gods, but also the creation of an image of Him that suits our desire but misses the truth of Who He is.

Religion has given us a false image of God, an image that has been used to destroy civilisations, enslaved many and caused untold atrocities in the world. This image, worse of all, has robbed us of having a true relationship with God and thus robbing us of our true identity as His children.

Jesus came to reveal the nature of God to us, and that is why He made the following statement in **John 17:6**:

"I have manifested Your name to the men whom You have given Me out of the world. They were Yours, You gave them to Me, and they have kept Your word." **(NKJV)**

What was this name Jesus was talking about? From the beginning of time, we knew God as *Elohim* – the creator. He further revealed Himself to Abraham as *Elshaddai* – the strong and breasted One, *Jehovah-Jireh* – the God that sees and provides, and other names. At the point Israel was to be delivered from the bondage of Egypt, He revealed Himself as *YHWH* – the I am and *Adonai* – Lord Master. Both names merged to create the compound name *Jehovah*. When He revealed Himself by this name to Moses, He made it clear to him that his fathers before him have never known Him by this name. In the same vein, when Jesus came, He revealed another name of God – Father. If you study every reference Jesus made to God, it was only on two occasions that He referred to God as God. Every other time, He referred to Him as Father. I believe this is the case because God's revelation to the Church is that He is Father.

The Church, however, has not come to terms with the implication of this truth and that is why we still have a false perception of God. God loves us like a Father loves His children. His nature, identity and the entirety of His being are wrapped up in this one word, Father. For this reason, I believe that when Jesus taught the disciples to pray, He started with "Our Father..." Further to this, when He was about to be crucified, He told His disciples that whatever they ask the "Father" in His name. He did not say Jehovah, or Elshaddai or Adonai or any other name, but Father. This is the only name we need to know God by, Father. Every other name gives contexts to the meaning of His fatherhood towards us.

The Knowledge of True Biblical Doctrine and Worship

Nothing has divided the Church more than the issue of doctrine and worship. In fact, denominations are formed based on the type of doctrine and mode of worship they subscribe to. For example:

Baptists do not believe the manifestation of the gifts of the Holy Spirit in today's Church

- **Pentecostals** believe in the manifestation of the gifts of the Holy Spirit

- **Seventh Day Adventists** see Saturday as the Sabbath Day and should be the day of worship

- **The Aladura Denomination** – the first Pente-charismatic denomination believe in the power of the Holy Spirit, they dress in a uniform for worship (the white garment), and some sects within the denomination believe in ritualistic elements to worship. They also subscribe to some of the laws under the Aaronic priesthood, such as not allowing women to come to Church during their menstrual cycle and do not let them sit in the Church altar or lead the service for the same reason

While most of these denominational beliefs have some footing in scripture, these questions come to mind:

- Why do these denominational differences seem to conflict with each other theologically?

- Why have they caused so much strife within the Church?

- Are some right and others wrong?

Throughout most of Jesus' ministry, He encountered the same doctrinal strife. There was a time when the disciples of John accused the disciples of Jesus of not fasting, and Jesus responded:

*"Can the friends of the bridegroom mourn as long as the bridegroom is with them? But the days will come when the bridegroom will be taken away from them, and then they will fast. No one puts a piece of unshrunk cloth on an old garment; for the patch pulls away from the garment, and the tear is made worse. Nor do they put new wine into old wineskins, or else the wineskins break, the wine is spilled, and the wineskins are ruined. But they put new wine into new wineskins, and both are preserved." (*MATTHEW *9: 15 – 17 NKJV)*

I remember as a young Christian when I stumbled on this passage; I struggled to understand it. At that time, what I believe the Holy Spirit explained to me about mixing the unshrunk cloth and old cloth and pouring new wine in old wineskin is mixing the Old Covenant and New Covenant. But now, the influence of the Holy Spirit, I see that this was a lesser truth, it is true, but lesser – just as the moon is a lesser light to the sun. What I believe the Holy Spirit is saying at this time is that it was not just a case of Old Testament and New Testament, but a matter of dispensations.

Dispensations refer to times and seasons. If we read what Jesus said carefully, you will notice that the primary subject of His statement was time. He did not say that fasting or not fasting in itself is wrong, but He did say is that it is a matter of time and season, just as Solomon explains in **Ecclesiastes chapter 3**.

This same theme appears in His conversation with the Samaritan woman at the well of Jacob, when she asked whose mode of worship was right: the Samaritans who believe they have to worship at Mount Gerizim or the Jews who believe they have to worship at Jerusalem. Jesus responded:

"Woman, believe Me, the **hour** *is coming when you will neither on this mountain nor in Jerusalem, worship the Father. You worship what you do not know; we know what we worship, for salvation is of the Jews. But the* **hour** *is coming, and now is, when the true worshipers will worship the Father in spirit and truth; for the Father is seeking such to worship Him. God is Spirit, and those who worship Him must worship in spirit and truth."* **(John 4: 21 – 24 NKJV)**

The word "**hour**" was mentioned twice in this statement that Jesus made to this woman. Therefore, based on this and scriptures from the Old Testament, there was a time when worshipping on Mount Gerizim at Shechem was right, and at another time, Jerusalem became the right place to worship after David conquered Jerusalem and his son – Solomon built the temple there. Now the time has come where it does not matter where you worship, but that you worship in spirit and truth. By this, Jesus was saying, *"know the right doctrine for the current dispensation."*

There are seven dispensations:

- **The dispensation of Innocence** – this was before the fall of humanity, while they were still in the Garden of Eden, basking in the presence of God.

- **The dispensation of Sin and Death** – this was after the fall of man. Wickedness ruled in the Earth and sin and death came into the world. This was the time between Adam and Moses.

- **The dispensation of the Law** – this was when God revealed Himself to Moses and gave the law to him and the children of Israel. The law was given to reveal the effect of the previous dispensation and to show humanities need for God.

- **The dispensation of Grace and Truth**– this started at the beginning of Jesus' ministry. The Bible says that the law came by Moses, but grace and truth came by Jesus Christ (**JOHN 1:17**). This dispensation was fully established when Jesus died on the cross, rose from the dead and sent the Holy Spirit to establish the Church. This is the dispensation we are in today; it is the dispensation that was described by the writer of **HEBREWS** when he said *"we have not come to Mount Sinai with smokes, fires and thundering; we have come to Mount Zion, the city of living to God. To a myriad of angels in festivity and God Himself is there"* (**HEBREWS 12: 18 – 22** – PARAPHRASED AND EMPHASIS ADDED). I believe we are on the last leg of this dispensation. I also believe that the revival being released on the Earth will lead to the next dispensation.

- **The dispensation of Suffering** – this will be the time of the great tribulation when the Church will be handed over to Satan to be tempted, and the anti-Christ will rule the Earth, cause great havoc and deceive many – leading them to eternal damnation. The Principalities of darkness will be in full manifestation at this time, but the good news is that I know by the Holy Spirit that there will still be angelic activities during this dispensation. This dispensation is usually joined with the dispensation of grace because many believe that people can still be saved at this time. While this is true because Jesus said "those who endure to the end will be saved" (Matthew 24:13), it is important to separate this dispensation as it is very key in the world calendar.

- **The dispensation of Judgment** – this happens simultaneously with the latter part of the dispensation of suffering. In this dispensation, the judgment of God will come on the Earth. He will judge the anti-Christ and pour out seven woes on the Earth, which some scholars believe will be as a result of the prayers of the Church. This dispensation ends with the second coming of Jesus Christ. The anti-Christ and the false prophets will be cast into the lake of fire and Satan will be thrown into the bottomless pit for one thousand years.

- **The dispensation of Glory** – this is the reign of Jesus Christ. It is known as the millennial reign. This is when the Church will reign with Jesus, and those who lived by faith during the previous dispensation will be in places of authority. They will rule over cities and regions with Christ. The end of this dispensation will be marked by the release of Satan from the bottomless pit to tempt the world again. He will gather an army against the Lord Jesus and will be cast into the lake of fire. After this follows judgment day, where those who supported the anti-Christ, the false prophets and Satan are sent into the lake of fire. Hell and Death are also sent into the lake of fire. What follows after this is the new beginning, the coming of the new Earth, void of Satan and all his angels; void of sin and wickedness. The Bible says that there will be no need for a temple or light because God will be our temple (**REVELATIONS 21: 22 – 23**).

The chronicles of the dispensations show that our approach to God changes depending on the dispensation we are in. In this dispensation of grace, we are not under the requirements of the law. However, when trying to mix the dispensation of law with the dispensation of grace, it brings confusion, conflict, and destruction. This was the issue that Jesus dealt with during His ministry on the Earth, the Pharisees, Sadducees and other religious leaders did not want to admit that they had entered a new dispensation. This same problem spilled over into the Church, even amongst those who believed. After Paul had preached the gospel to Gentiles, some Jewish Christians, who were described as members of the sect of circumcision, began to teach the Gentiles that except they are circumcised, they could not be saved. The matter was brought to the council of elders in Jerusalem, and they had a heated debate about what should be the right doctrine for the Church, especially the Gentile Church. Then the Apostle Peter, leader of the council stood up and said:

"Men and brethren, you know that a good while ago God chose among us, that by my mouth the Gentiles should hear the word of the gospel and believe. So God, who knows the heart, acknowledged them by giving them the Holy Spirit, just as

He did *to us, and made no distinction between them and us, purifying their hearts by faith. Now therefore, why do you test God by putting a yoke on the neck of the disciples which neither our fathers nor we were able to bear? But we believe that through the grace of the Lord Jesus Christ we shall be saved in the same manner as they."* (Acts 15: 7 – 11 NKJV)

This statement led to a long silence and the council listened to the testimonies of Barnabas and Paul of the workings of miracles by the power of the Holy Spirit and how many Gentiles had come to believe in Jesus Christ. Following this, Apostle James, the half-brother of Jesus, stood up and said:

"Men and brethren, listen to me: Simon has declared how God at first visited the Gentiles to take out of them a people for His name. And with this the words of the prophets agree, just as it is written: 'After this I will return and will rebuild the tabernacle of David, which has fallen down; I will rebuild its ruins, and I will set it up; so that the rest of mankind may seek the Lord, even all the Gentiles who are called by My name, says the Lord who does all these things.'

"Known to God from eternity are all His works. Therefore I judge that we should not trouble those from among the Gentiles who are turning to God, but that we write to them to abstain from things polluted by idols, from sexual immorality, from things strangled, and from blood. For Moses has had throughout many generations those who preach him in every city, being read in the synagogues every Sabbath." (Acts 15: 13 – 21 NKJV)

This statement led to the council writing to the Gentile Church, listing everything James said as a doctrine for them and asking them not to listen to those trying to burden them with circumcision.

Studying the discussion, they had then; you will see that through the reasoning of the scriptures, they were able to determine that they were now in the dispensation of grace as mentioned first by Peter and then James, the half-brother of Jesus. The question, therefore, is that if they could agree, why can't we?

There are three reasons why I believe they were able to come to this agreement:

- **They recognised the Lordship and Partnership of the Holy Spirit (Acts 15:28)** – this was demonstrated in how they expressed their decision to the Gentle Church; they put the Holy Spirit ahead of themselves. Sadly, we the Church of today put our thoughts first and try to fit the Holy Spirit into it.

- **They focused on the Scriptures (Acts 15: 15 – 17)** – when James cited the scripture that highlighted the gospel being preached to the Gentiles, it ended all arguments. Therefore, they filtered their opinions and thoughts through the Word and not the Word, through their thoughts.

- **They gathered in one accord (Acts 15:25)** – though they had their disagreements, they were submitted to one another, respected each other and focused on establishing the truth, rather than their own opinions.

The reason why the Church of today cannot do what the early Church did is that we are more focused on being right, than establishing the truth. We have the same problem the religious leaders had when Jesus was on the Earth. We simply do not care about the truth; we only care about followership and posterity that we cannot see that our arrogance is destroying the very future we are trying to protect. The only way to deal with our differences and conflict is not to try to convince each other of our standpoint and biases, but to first abandon our theology and seek the truth. However, we cannot honestly know the truth nor walk in it, except by partnering with the Holy Spirit.

Chapter 5
The Spirit and the Church

Though the concept of the Trinity is one of the causes of contention in the Church, because the word itself is not mentioned once in the Bible, the concept of Trinity is nevertheless one of the foundations of Christianity. This is because the Bible says that there are Three Who testify in Heaven, the Father, the Word, and the Spirit. These Three testify to the divinity of Jesus Christ and that He died and rose from the dead to give salvation to humanity. Therefore, to deny the Trinity is to deny Christianity and the Trio are described in several parts of the Bible as the Godhead.

Further to this, the Trinity or the Godhead have been in manifestation from the beginning of time. The Bible says that God created the Heavens and the Earth. The Hebrew word for "**God**" in this context is "***Elohim***," which is the plurality of the Hebrew word "***Eloha***" (**GENESIS 1:1**). Therefore, when the Bible says God created the Heavens and the Earth, what was being said was that the Godhead created the Heavens and Earth. So, the work of creation was as a result of a partnership between the Father, Word, and Spirit.

The following two verses further shows the individual role of the Trinity:

"The Earth was without form and void; and darkness was on the face of the deep. And the Spirit of God was hovering over the face of the waters.

"Then God said, "Let there be light"; and there was light. And God saw the light, that it was good; and God divided the light from the darkness." (**GENESIS 1: 2 – 3 NKJV**)

The first person of Trinity introduced to us individually is the Holy Spirit; He is known as the active presence of God, or rather, God in action. We see His action demonstrated here as He hovered over the waters, redeeming the Earth from the powers of darkness as explained in **Chapter 1**.

The next thing we notice is that God said, which means we are introduced to His Word. The Word of God is a Person, as we further understand in Genesis 3 when the Bible says that Adam and Eve heard the Voice of God walking in the Garden (**verse 8**). We find again in **John 1:1** when the Word was re-introduced to us as God and in **verse 14**, as Jesus. **Colossians 1:15** describes the Word, which is Jesus, as:

- The express image of God, the Father

- The Head of all creation

- He made all things – so He is the Creator

These descriptions establish the Word as the manifestation of God. Jesus Himself confirmed this when He told Philip that when they see Him, they have seen the Father (**John 14:8**).

In These Two, we see the essence of the Father – Who is regarded as the centre point of the Godhead. He is God enthroned.

The Manifestations of God on the Earth

During the dispensation of sin and the law, the most seemingly active member of the Godhead is the Lord, Who was later described to us as Father by Jesus. However, it is my opinion that it was only during the procession of the children of Israel to the Promised Land that we see the actual manifestation of the Father on the Earth. I say this for two reasons:

- **God physically manifested on His throne on Mount Sinai.** One instance where this was made evident was when God asked Moses to bring the elders of Israel to the Mountain (**Exodus 24: 9 – 11**). The Bible says that they looked upon the Lord of Host and He did not kill them. I believe that they looked into the throne room of God and they saw God sitting on the throne. That is God the Father.

- **The Ark of the Covenant Represents the throne of God.** The Bible says that God is enthroned between the Cherubim (**2 Samuel 6:2, Psalm 99:1, Isaiah 37:16**) and the Ark of Covenant had two golden Cherubs facing each other on the cover of the Ark. This cover is known as the mercy seat, which covered the law that was placed inside the Ark. Therefore, the Ark of Covenant was a prototype of the throne of God. God showed Moses a prototype of His throne and commanded Him to make a copy - so when the children of Israel saw the throne, they would see God amongst them. This is why I believe that God commanded that the Ark must be carried on the shoulders of the priests as if carrying a throne because that was what it was. To further prove this, the Bible mentioned several times that God spoke to Moses from between of the Cherubim (**Exodus 25:22, Numbers 7:89**).

However, apart from this time, all the other manifestation of God was not God the Father, but the Holy Spirit. He was the Person responsible for the raising of the Judges, the ministry of the Prophets and He was the anointing that came upon the kings of Israel.

Another fact about the Holy Spirit is that He is the Father of Jesus Christ because He was the One Who came on Mary and planted Jesus in her womb (**Luke 1:35**). Jesus confirmed this when He said, *"it is My Father Who works in Me that does these works"* (**John 14:10**). In that same vein, He is our Father.

It is essential to understand this, so we know that the Holy Spirit did not show up on the Earth on the day of Pentecost in **Acts 2**. He was always here and manifested the presence of God through all the chosen instruments of the Lord. The only difference between that dispensation and this is that He has come to the Earth in His fullness. This is why Jesus said that the Father had given the Spirit to the Son without measure (**John 3:34**) and He also said that in the same way the Father sent Him, so He sends us (**John 20:21**). When Jesus said in the same way, He meant it in every sense. Therefore, just as the Father gave Jesus the Holy Spirit without measure, so He has given us the Holy Spirit without measure. Thus, the Holy Spirit is available to us – individual, in the same way, He was available to Jesus when He was on the Earth. However, for us to experience the Holy Spirit, we need to relate to Him as Jesus did.

Jesus' Relationship with the Holy Spirit

Five key events or dispensations of Jesus' life gives us an indication of how Jesus relates to the Holy Spirit:

- His Baptism

- His Temptation in the wilderness

- His Ministry

- The time leading to His Crucifixion

- After His Resurrection

His Baptism

The Holy Spirit was responsible for baptising Jesus Christ, and He was the One Who qualified Jesus as the Christ. The sign that was given to John Baptist by which he will know the Anointed One, was the One on Whom the Holy Spirit descends on (**JOHN 1: 32 – 34**). Therefore, the Holy Spirit was the anointing of Jesus' life.

His Temptation in the wilderness

After the baptism and the utterance of God the Father, confirming that Jesus is His Son, the next thing we see is that the Holy Spirit led Jesus to the wilderness to be tempted by the Devil. The operative word here is **"led."** He was the One reminding Jesus of the scriptures to counteract the temptations of Satan. This means that Holy Spirit trained Jesus and consequently, Jesus was completely surrendered to Him, unless The Holy Spirit will not have led him.

His Ministry

In **JOHN 14:10**, we see that the Holy Spirit was the One doing the works through Jesus and that He referred to Him as Father. Therefore, Jesus saw the Holy Spirit as higher than Him. So, we see that the Holy Spirit was Jesus' Senior Partner in ministry. Jesus followed the lead of the Holy Spirit. This is why He also said that He could do nothing of Himself, but He does what He sees His Father do, and says what He hears His Father say (**JOHN 5:19**). The Holy Spirit was the Father Jesus was referring to.

Therefore, everything Jesus did or said was by the Holy Spirit.

The time leading to His Crucifixion

At this point, when Jesus was about to die for the sins of the world and be glorified, we see Him speak of the Holy Spirit almost as a servant or a subordinate, because He said that He would send the

Holy Spirit. However, to fully understand what Jesus was saying let's review the exact words He said:

"Nevertheless I tell you the truth. It is to your advantage that I go away; for if I do not go away, the Helper will not come to you; but if I depart, I will send Him to you... I still have many things to say to you, but you cannot bear them now. However, when He, the Spirit of truth, has come, He will guide you into all truth; for He will not speak on His own authority, but whatever He hears He will speak; and He will tell you things to come. He will glorify Me, for He will take of what is Mine and declare it to you. All things that the Father has are Mine. Therefore I said that He will take of Mine and declare it to you." (JOHN 16: 7; 12 – 15 NKJV)

The word **"send"** is from the Greek word *"pempo,"* which to dispatch – to release or allow. If we read the word in the full context of Jesus' statement, you will see that what He was saying that He leaving allows the Holy Spirit to come. So, it is not as if He is sending the Holy Spirit as a messenger, even though that itself can be true, because the Godhead submits to each other, but that in submission to the plan of the Godhead from the beginning of time, after the work of Jesus on the Earth was complete, the Holy Spirit would be released as prophesied in the book of **JOEL 2:17**.

Another reason why the Holy Spirit may be subordinate to Jesus is that He said *"He will not speak on His authority, but whatever He hears He will speak; and He will tell you things to come. He will glorify Me, for He will take of what is Mine and declare it to you."* However, if we remember, Jesus said the same thing about Himself, which He only says what the Father says and from what we have discussed previously, we see that Jesus was talking about the Holy Spirit when He referred to the Father. Therefore, when Jesus said, *"He will take of what is Mine and declare it to you,"*

He goes further to explain, *"All things that the Father has are Mine. Therefore I said that He would take of Mine and declare it to you."* Knowing Jesus referred to Holy Spirit as Father, we can deduce that what Jesus was in effect saying is that He and the Holy Spirit are One. Therefore, Jesus was unified with the Holy Spirit in purpose and identity.

Further to this, Jesus wanted us to see something even more significant. If you notice, everything Jesus said He would send the Holy Spirit to do was all the things He had experienced the Holy Spirit do for Him. Therefore, Jesus wanted us to see that just as the Holy Spirit related to Him while He was on Earth, so will He relate to us, also.

"If you love Me, keep My commandments. And I will pray for the Father, and He will give you another Helper, that He may abide with you forever— the Spirit of truth, whom the world cannot receive because it neither sees Him nor knows Him; but you know Him, for He dwells with you and will be in you. I will not leave you orphans; I will come to you." (JOHN 14: 15 – 18 NKJV)

The scripture above encapsulate all that Jesus wants us to know about the Holy Spirit as He experienced Him during His ministry on the Earth:

- **Helper** – from the Greek word **"*parakletos*,"** which means advocate, counselor and if I may add a guide

- **The Spirit of Truth** – this means He will be our Teacher and just as He led Jesus and revealed the truth to Him, He will come to us, also

- **He will be in us** – in the same way, the Holy Spirit was in Jesus and was the anointing that worked in Him; He is the anointing that is at work in us, also

- **Will not leave us as orphans** – the Greek word for orphans in this text is *"orphanos,"* which means comfortless or without a father. Therefore, just as Jesus called Him Father, so can we. Because He too has become our Father

After His Resurrection

After Jesus' resurrection, He told His disciples not to do anything until they had received the Holy Spirit. He described Him as the power from on high. What Jesus was, in fact, saying here is that, just like Him, we cannot do anything except by the Holy Spirit, a truth that the Church has sadly ignored.

Working with the Holy Spirit

Jesus showed us that the Holy Spirit is the power of God and is in fact, God. The early Church knew this and accorded the Holy Spirit this regard. They recognised that the Holy Spirit is the founder and Lord of the Church. They worked in full partnership with Him and wholly surrendered to His leading. For example:

- **Ananias and Saphira (ACTS 5: 1 – 11)** – when this couple decided to deceive Apostles, by withholding part of the proceeds of their land which they sold and presenting the rest as the whole, Peter made it clear to them that they had lied to the Holy Spirit; they had not lied to men but God. The Holy Spirit judged the couple and killed them

- **He commanded Peter to go to the house of Cornelius (ACTS 10: 19 – 20)** – even after Jesus had commanded His disciples to make disciples of nations, they only preached to their Jewish brothers. However, at this point, after showing Peter a vision and inspiring

Cornelius to send for Peter through the visitation of an Angel, the Holy Spirit commanded Peter to follow the men who came from Cornelius, because He sent them. Therefore, this means that the Holy Spirit was responsible for sending the Angel. The Holy Spirit commanded Peter to go and admonished him not to doubt at all

- **Calling Barnabas and Paul to be Apostles to the Gentiles (ACTS 13:2)** – while the prophets and teachers gathered and ministered unto the Lord, the Holy Spirit commanded that Barnabas and Saul (whose name changed to Paul) to be separated unto Him for the work of the ministry He has called them

- **Giving doctrine to the Gentile Church (ACTS 15: 28 – 29)** – after discussing in one accord about the doctrine that the Gentile Church should follow, this was how they communicated their decision, *"For it seemed good to the Holy Spirit, and to us, to lay upon you no greater burden than these necessary things"*. Notice that they put the Holy Spirit first, which indicates that they recognise Him as the senior partner in their decision

These examples show that the authority the Holy Spirit had over the early the Church. Sadly, the Church of this age does not seem to have the same sensitivity and submission to the Holy Spirit. It is no wonder the Church is so fractured and powerless.

The Holy Spirit is the Potter

God is molding His Church. When God sent Jeremiah to the house of the Potter **(JEREMIAH 18: 1 – 4)**:

"The word which came to Jeremiah from the LORD, saying: "Arise and go down to the potter's house, and there I will cause you to hear My words." Then I went down to the potter's house, and there he was, making something at the wheel. And the vessel that he made of clay was marred in the hand of the potter; so he made it again into another vessel, as it seemed good to the potter to make." **(NKJV)**

This is what I hear the Spirit saying at this time:

> **"I am the Potter sayeth the Lord, and I make My vessels in the shape that suit My purpose and will. For those that resist Me, I will utterly cast out. Only those who surrender to Me shall be of use to Me in the revival I am sending on the Earth."**

I sense an urge from the Holy Spirit to emphasise that He is the Potter. The Holy Spirit is the Potter. He is not the instrument or the tool. We are the tools and instruments in His hand. It is the lack of this understanding that has kept the Church at bay for too long. We have relegated the work of the ministry to business strategies and administrative prowess. While these have their place and are very important – even inspired by the Holy Spirit, they must be deployed within the context of His leading. But sadly, it seems we are the ones wanting to lead the Holy Spirit. However, those who will be led by Him in this season will be the ones who will be His instrument in the revival He is about to release on the Earth this year.

Will you allow yourself to be led by Him?

Chapter 6
The Children and Heirs

God has called us His children. John had this incredible revelation about the Church, when he stated, *"Now are we children of God..."* (1 JOHN 3:2). We are not just believers, followers or servants; we are children.

We are children and heirs of God, joint heirs with our Lord Jesus. However, though we can lay the same claim to all the riches of God as Jesus can, these riches are not available to every Christian, even though it is every Christian's birthright.

So why is this the case? The answer to this question is that there are two kinds of children that God has; **nepios** and **uihos**.

The Nepios

"Now I say that *the heir, as long as he is a child, does not differ at all from a slave, though he is master of all, but is under guardians and stewards until the time appointed by the father."* (GALATIANS 4:1 NKJV)

The word **"child"** in the original Greek text is the word **"nepios."** This word means; **infant**, **babbler** and **a simple person** - who Strong's Concordance further describes as an immature Christian.

Imagine a wealthy man, who lives in a state of the art mansion and has untold wealth to his name. He and his wife produced a beautiful baby, one who was destined to inherit all that they amassed for themselves. However, as long as that child remains a child, he will still need someone to tell when to eat and what he can eat. He will still need to ask for permission to play in the garden. He will still need to ask for money from his parents and justify why he needs it. He can't drive the cars except his parents deem it appropriate for him to do so. Even the stewards who work for him are still in the position to instruct and correct him. Though everything belongs to him, he does not have access to them; he does not differ from a servant.

This is where many Christians are today. They are **nepios.** They have not come into maturity. Therefore, though everything belongs to them, they do not have access to it and subject to the same elemental forces that unbelievers are, such as; envy, anger, murderous rage, irritability, sexual immorality and all forms of evil.

But imagine if the child described in the analogy above, decides to lay claim to his inheritance – while he is still a child, what do you think will happen? Imagine if he decides to instruct one of the stewards, drive the car, or access money that was not made available to him – what do you think will happen to him? He will likely create a mess and be strongly reprimanded by his parents and even the stewards who work for him. He may even be treated as a thief because he has taken what was not made available to him – even though they are his to inherit.

Sadly, this is a big problem the Church is facing today. **Nepios** are trying to act like grown-ups, and some of them are leading Churches, standing on pulpits or in the Church leadership. It is no wonder that the Church is so dysfunctional. What else should we expect when children interact with each other – they will fight, right? What makes it worse is that there are hardly any adults to stop the fighting and send them to the naughty corner. Sadder still, is when the Holy Spirit sends adults amongst these children, their false sense of maturity (perhaps because of their professional success, age, theological training, years of being in the Church or being a Christian, or esoteric experiences) causes them to ignore and sometimes, even persecute these adults sent to help them grow up. These groups are the most prominent problem of the Church, they have caused many to lose faith in God, and it is because of them that many blaspheme God.

It is, for this reason, James said not everyone should become teachers, because teachers receive the harshest form of punishment from God (**James 3:1**). Paul instructed Timothy not to be too quick to anoint people into the position of leadership, especially those who are new to the faith – these he instructed not to anoint at all so that they are not puffed up with pride (**1 Timothy 5:22, 1 Timothy 3:6**). Sadly, the Church has ignored these warnings. Today, most people are appointed to places of authority because of nepotism. It is either they are a relation of the Church leader or because of the material contributions they can or have made to the Church; instead of maturity and service.

These *nepios* need to sit down and learn. This is the position they are supposed to be until they become adults and are ready to take the responsibilities God has prepared for them. To take this responsibility prematurely will only cause untold damage to the Church and the world.

The Uihos

"For as many as are led by the Spirit of God, these are sons of God." (**Romans 8:14 NKJV**)

The word **"sons"** in the original Greek text was the word, *"uihos,"* which represents those who have come into maturity. I say this because the word is mainly used to describe Jesus (except **John 17:12**, when Jesus was referring to the son of perdition).

Another reason why I say this is because the scripture above shows us that what qualifies these Christians to be called *uihos* is that the Holy Spirit leads them.

In chapter 3, we discussed the qualifying factor of becoming a child of God, which is to believe in Jesus (**JOHN 1: 12 – 13**). The word **"children"** in this scripture was expressed as the word, *"teknon"* in the original Greek text; which means offspring. It is what we refer to as the new birth. *Teknon* is the same word used in **1 JOHN 3:2** when John was talking to all Church. Therefore, every Christian is a *teknon*, because we are all offspring of God.

However, after reading **ROMANS 8:14**, you will discover that a different qualification is required to be called a *uihos*. They need to be led by the Holy Spirit.

Studying the life of Jesus (part of which we discussed in **CHAPTER 5**), you will discover that **ROMANS 8:14** summed up the life of Jesus. The Holy Spirit led him. Following the criterion provided in this verse, we can see that this was what gave Him the right to be called the Son of God. This is especially true because before He was baptised by the Holy Spirit (except for the prophecy of His birth), He was never referred to as the Son of God, only the boy Jesus.

These are the Christians that God is looking for, those through which God can demonstrate His might and power (**2 CHRONICLES 16:9**). They are the champions of God.

A Call to Sonship

Many years ago, while in a Fellowship, I attend every Tuesday called *Saving A Generation Endangered (SAGE)*, the Spirit of the Lord spoke to me:

> **"Arise to the place of sonship; I am the Father you have always been looking for."**

When I received this word from God, I thought it was to comfort me, because I did not have the best relationship with my father and as a result, I looked to mentors for the support a son should receive from his father. But after a while, the Lord showed me that sonship is not just a relationship, but a place and position of authority. The Lord told me that as a son, He would do things for others because I asked Him to.

Did you know that this was what Jesus experienced at the tomb of Lazarus and the wedding at Cana? These miracles where done, because Jesus asked them of the Father and the Father never holds anything away from His sons. These are the ones he referred to as the adoption – *"uihothesia."* They are called the adoption because God has specifically and purposefully chosen and trained them by the Holy Spirit. They have, through reason of use (practice) have learnt to discern what is right and wrong (**HEBREWS 5:14**). These are the ones who can manifest the glory of God and operate in their inheritance – even on the Earth, just as Jesus did.

The call to sonship is for every Christian. Just as every child as the potential to become an adult, so also, every **nepios** can become a **uihos**, but this can only happen when we learn to submit to the Lordship of the Holy Spirit – to be surrendered to, taught and led by Him, just as Jesus. Until we learn to do this, we cannot access our inheritance in God, and we will be no different as unbelievers – we will die just like the princes and the men of the world (**PSALMS 82:7**).

Chapter 7
The Manifestation of the Sons of God

God, just as creation, is earnestly looking forward to the manifestation of His sons. This is why the Bible says that God is standing in the Council of gods. He is waiting for His sons to take their place and subdue the Earth as He planned from the beginning. To subdue the Earth implies bringing to a halt the chaos unleashed on the Earth by other humans who are under the influence of Satan.

I remember watching one of the episodes of the series *"Once Upon a Time."* In this series, two men were in a wilderness, under the scorching sun and dying of thirst. In their search for water, they saw a cup (which represented the Holy Grail) on a rock, and at first thought, it was a mirage. One of the men, only concerned about quenching his thirst ran towards the cup, grabbed it and was destroyed by it. The second, though afraid about his comrade's fate, still followed suit; except before grabbing the cup, he acknowledged the miracle and drank from the cup and was momentarily refreshed. However, something stranger than the appearance of a cup in the wilderness happened. After drinking from the cup, he turned around to recline on the rock for a respite. To his shock, as he placed his hand on the ground, the barren wilderness was instantaneously covered with green pastures.

This scene gave me a picture of what God meant when He said through the Prophet Isaiah:

Until the Spirit is poured upon us from on high, and the wilderness becomes a fruitful field, and the fruitful field is counted as a forest. (ISAIAH 32:15 NKJV)

Just as the man received the miracle of the cup in the wilderness and by drinking of it, he was able to change the desolation of the wilderness into a fruitful field, in the same way we have received the Holy Spirit and can now transform the desolate heritages and bring order to the Earth, just as Jesus said:

"But you shall receive power when the Holy Spirit has come upon you, and you shall be witnesses to Me in Jerusalem, and in all Judea and Samaria, and to the end of the earth." **(ACTS 1:8 NKJV)**

For many years, I had thought that the coming of the Holy Spirit would turn the wilderness of into a fruitful field. I thought it was God that will do the transformation. I thought I was supposed to wait on God to transform my life. This thought was true at the beginning. In chapter 1, we discussed how the world was in a desolate state and utter chaos, but the Holy Spirit hovered over the surface of the deep, restoring order and creating the groundwork for the restoration of the Earth. However, in this dispensation, this is no longer true. The Holy Spirit is not doing the transformation as He did in **GENESIS 1:2**, because He has given the Earth as an inheritance to us humans. Nevertheless, knowing we cannot do it by ourselves, He has instilled in us that, through His presence in our lives, we can do what He did at the beginning – to bring chaos to order and restore the Earth. Therefore, Jesus says that when the Holy Spirit comes upon us we will receive power. The power to bear witness to what He has done to redeem the creation. He has given us the power to unleash His blessing on the Earth. It is, therefore, through us that the wilderness will be transformed into a fruitful field.

There are many examples of people through whom the Holy Spirit has restored order to the Earth or parts of the Earth. One of them was Abraham, whom God blessed, saying, through you the nations of the Earth shall be blessed. The fullness of this prophecy was manifested in Jesus Christ, but it also manifested in some of his descendants before Christ:

- **Isaac** sowed in famine and reaped a hundred-fold

- **Jacob,** after Laban deceived him, received wisdom from God to overcome his deceit and became very wealthy as a result. Another example is when Jacob blessed Pharaoh. We understand from scripture that the one who blesses is greater than the one whom he blesses. This is why the order of Melchizedek is higher than the priesthood of Aaron, because Levi, the tribe from which Aaron came was in the loins of Abraham when he was blessed by Melchizedek (**HEBREWS 7: 7 – 10**). In the same vein, when Jacob blessed Pharaoh, he recognised that as the custodian of the Abrahamic blessing, he is higher than the throne of Pharaoh – the most powerful man in the world. Jacob was so conscious of this reality that he blessed Pharaoh twice and guess what? Pharaoh let him

- **Joseph** rose from a slave to become the governor of Egypt. It is not the rise to power that was significant, but that he rose to power to save the world from famine. No wise man in the most developed civilisation of that era could solve the riddle of Pharaoh's dream, until Joseph. His solving of the mystery and his idea to address the threat that it posed prevented Egypt from desolation and preserved the known world. God raise Joseph to become a god to Egypt

- **Moses** survived the cruel order of the Pharaoh of his time and grew up as a prince in the palace of the same Pharaoh. He watched from afar his people suffer from the bondage and oppression of the Egyptians. However, when it was time for God to deliver Israel from captivity, He said to Moses, *"I will make you as God unto Pharaoh..."* (EXODUS 4:16; 7:1). It was by the word of Moses that signs and wonders were done in Egypt until the children of Israel were set free. So, God made Moses a god to Pharaoh and Egypt

- **Samuel** grew up under the tutorage of Eli to become a prophet in Israel. The Bible says that God confirmed every word that came out of his mouth so that it would be known that there was a Prophet in Israel (**1 SAMUEL 3:19**). God used him to anoint the first two kings of Israel. God made him His oracle to Israel

- **David**, the greatest king Israel ever had, grew up as the rejected son of Jesse and abandoned to carter for a flock of sheep and wrestle with bears and lions when they attacked his flock. Some years after being anointed by Samuel as the replacement for Saul (who had sinned against God), he encountered Goliath, who terrified and defiled the army of Israel. He stepped up to confront the giant and defeated the champion of the Philistines. Therefore, God made him a god to the Philistines, and during his reign, God delivered Israel entirely from the hand of the Philistines and brought the children of Israel to their full inheritance

- **Solomon** became the wisest king that ever existed unto Jesus Christ. God brought nations to his footsteps, and so he became a god to nations

- **Elijah** was a mysterious fellow who just surfaced to the scene without any clear background. All we know about him is that he is from Tishbe in Gilead, east of the Jordan River in what was is known as Jordan today. His first appearance was when he appeared in the palace of Ahab to announce a three and half year drought. There was no build up recorded, just straight up drama. He became a terror to the house of Ahab and killed four hundred and fifty prophets of Baal in a battle of gods standoff. God made him a god to the house of Ahab and like a god to Israel

- **Elisha**, the businessman turn prophet served under Elijah as his apprentice and took over from him when he was caught up into Heaven in a whirlwind. His first act as a prophet was dividing the River Jordan in two, with the mantle of his predecessor. He became the leading prophet of Israel, and his influence was so strong that the king once referred to him as his father. Elisha through divine inspiration revealed the secret plans of the king of Syria against Israel, and as a result, he sent an entire army against Elisha. God and Elisha blinded these armies and led them to the king of Israel's palace, where they were disarmed and sent back to their king in peace. This brought temporary peace between both nations. He was also recorded to have performed double the number of miracles his predecessor did and his dead bones raised someone to life. God made Elisha a god to Syria, the king of Israel and like a god to the people of Israel

- **Daniel,** who was part of the Jews taken captive to Babylon, rose to become one of the highest-ranking officers in the land that was supposed to enslave him. He was known to be the ten times wiser than the wisest men in the land (**DANIEL 1:20**). In one occasion, Nebuchadnezzar had a dream, which none of the wise men of the land could interpret. As a result, he ordered the killing of all the wise men in the land, but when they got to Daniel and his friends, Daniel was able to convince the captain to give him an audience with the king. Daniel and his friends sought God and were able to reveal to the king the dream and the interpretation of it to the king. This action saved the lives of the rest of the wise men in Babylon. Therefore, God made Daniel a god unto Babylon

- **Shadrach, Meshach, and Abed-Nego** were cornered by the king Nebuchadnezzar to worship the statue he had erected. Upon their refusal, he ordered for them to be thrown into the furnace of fire. Though the men who threw them in the furnace died, the three Hebrew men started walking free in the furnace, and a fourth person was found among them, which had the appearance of the Son of God. Nebuchadnezzar called hem out of the fire, a revival broke out and a new a decree was issued against anyone that will blaspheme the God of the three Hebrew men. Therefore, through their obedience, God made them a god unto Babylon

- **Nehemiah** was the cupbearer of the king of Persia until he heard the news about the desolation of Jerusalem. He made up his mind to rebuild the walls of Jerusalem, repair the ruins and restore what was once lost, even though he faced opposition from the people of the surrounding countries who despised anyone who had the well-being of Jerusalem at heart. Nehemiah still found favour with God and was appointed as the governor of Jerusalem. God made him like a god to the people of Jerusalem

All these men stood as gods in their generations; they were champions of God because they stood to be counted as men of principle, purpose, and compassion. These were the people God was referring to when He rebuked king Asa of Judah when he went to ally with a country God planned to give to him. All because he could not trust God to help him win a war against a nation who had fewer soldiers than the one million men army of the Ethiopians he defeated by trusting God. God told Him that His eyes go throughout the Earth to find someone He can make Himself strong to (**2 Chronicles 16:9**). This scripture implies that God is looking for a man through whom He can show off, and He did through the names of the men mentioned above.

Though these great men did wonderful things and were used mightily by God, Jesus made a shocking statement about them when He was referring to John the Baptist:

***"Assuredly, I say to you, among those born of women there has not risen one greater than John the Baptist; but he who is least in the kingdom of heaven is greater than he."* (Matthew 11:11 NKJV)**

Jesus was saying two things here:

1. All these men were not as great as John the Baptist

2. John the Baptist cannot be compared to the least Christian in the Church

So, if we were to do a hierarchical structure based on Jesus' statement, it would look like this:

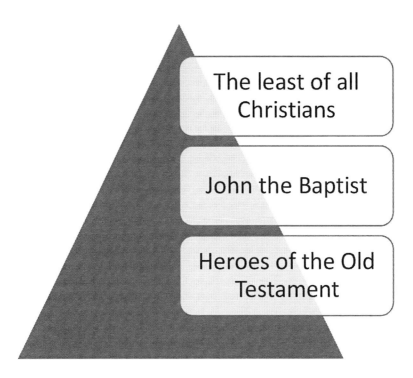

Going by the statement of Jesus, it means that at the very least, every Christian should outshine John the Baptist. So, the question is, why are we not even meeting the standards of the old prophets? Studying these characters, I identified three commonalities they shared, which I believe will help answer our question:

- They were first servants

- They had a vision

- They Partnered with the Holy Spirit

From these, I have coined the term, the **SVP Approach**, which stands for Service, Vision, and Partnership.

Service

Every one of these men started off serving someone or with a serving heart. Isaac served his father Abraham by surrendering himself to be killed by him while trusting God to provide an alternative sacrifice as his father said before they climbed the mountain. Jacob served his uncle Laban for twenty years, David served Saul, Elisha served Elijah. When Jehoshaphat heard that Elisha served Elijah, he was immediately convinced that God's word is with him. Therefore, Elisha's service to Elijah gave him credibility in the eye of the king of Judah (**2 KING 3: 11 – 12**). Samuel served Eli, Moses served Jethro as a Shepherd for forty years, Joshua was chosen to lead Israel after Moses because he served Moses, Nehemiah was a cupbearer – similar to the job of a waiter – to the king of Persia, and so on. These men developed the graces God put in their lives by serving others.

I remember hearing a story of a young man who felt God had called him to be a prophet. He spoke to a man of God about this wonderful ministry he felt God had called him to, but the man of God he spoke to shocked him by telling him to serve in his Church for six months. The young man was confused because he thought that the man of God would give him a pulpit. Instead, he got a broom – figuratively speaking. To my recollection, the young man did not take the opportunity of service.

It is so sad that most so-called leaders or aspiring leaders are like this young man mentioned – they do not understand the value of service and serving; it is no wonder they misbehave when they get to the position of leadership. Service or serving is essential because this is where the character is built, and it is a character that sustains purpose, not gifts and anointing. One can be anointed, but without the character of servitude as the foundation, that person's life will soon come crashing down.

If we consider ministers in recent history whose ministries are still flourishing today with limited scandals, you will see that they started off serving. Men of God like Pastor E. A. Adeboye – General Overseer of the Redeemed Church and John Bevere – Leader of Messenger International were once serving at another ministry. Pastor Adeboye served under the founder of the Church he is leading today – Pastor Josiah Akindayomi as an interpreter of English to Yoruba. There are several stories of how Pa Akindayomi would caution Pastor Adeboye publicly. The same is with John Bevere, who served as a chauffeur for ministers and served under Benny Hinn as the Youth Pastor of his Church before God called him into the ministry that he is in now.

This is a lesson that I have learnt, being in ministry for about twelve years serving under my Youth Pastor for eight years. If you cannot serve, you cannot lead, and therefore, **God cannot use you**. I have seen so many people in my generation make this mistake over and over again, and it is indeed heartbreaking, but I cannot blame them, because even the generations before us have made the same mistake. What scares me the most, however, is that the younger generation is making mistakes even at an alarming rate. They are too eager to take responsibilities and take leadership roles. While I am delighted at their enthusiasm, I am worried that they have not yet proved themselves in service and their eager pursuit of responsibility may be a recipe for disaster if not properly checked. Their fall may even be bigger and more devastating than the generations before them. It is so interesting that everybody wants to be a leader, but no one wants to serve, only if they understood that leadership is just a higher dimension of service.

Vision

Every one of these men had a vision or an ideal that was worth fighting for. God gave Abraham a vision of a land that He was taking him to, a land that generations after him would later possess and call their home. Moses was given the vision of the Promised Land and the emancipation of Israel from the bondage of Egypt. Daniel stood by what he was taught in the Torah and purposed in his heart not to defile himself by eating the unclean food served from the king's table. Elijah was so enraged by Israel's idolatry and the wicked rule of Ahab and Jezebel that he was moved to action, calling a three-and-a-half-year famine on the land. All these men stood for something, they believed in something. The question, therefore, is what do you stand for, what do you believe in, what enrages you, what keeps you awake at night? If you cannot answer these questions, then God has not yet called you and therefore, cannot use you.

One of the reasons I have experienced a measure of success in the ministry God has called me to serve in is because of the burning desire and overwhelming need to reach the people put in our care. This is why sometimes I will have the same ideas as the Youth Pastor because I am so soaked into the vision that we are almost operating at the same wavelength. However, his wavelength will always be higher than mine, because God will never speak to me as much as He will speak to him about the affairs of the Youth Fellowship. This is why if I have an idea that is in contrast with the vision God has given him, I back down immediately. Even if Jesus appears to me, and what He says goes against what my Youth Pastor has in his heart to do, then it must either be that the vision is not for this particular ministry, but for me to execute in the personal ministry that God is calling me to lead. Or, on the rare occasion that he is wrong, then the only thing I can do is intercede for him in prayer and leave it like that. Many anointed men and women of God have made the mistake of trying to coarse their Church leaders to do what they believe God has placed in their heart and as a result have become culprits of sedition in the Church. Most of the denominational splits have happened mainly because of a clash of vision or theological approach. Don't get me wrong, some of these splits were necessary, such as the Lutheran revolution, which came about because the papacy raised their authority above the Bible and thus, was leading the people away from God – an explicit form of apostasy. It is, therefore, only in the case of apostasy that sedition is necessary. If a leader is no longer leading his people to God, then those people need to stop following him, before they end up together with him in Hell.

Another mistake Christians make in the area of vision is mixing vision with ambition. While there is a fine line between the two, the difference is distinct enough to notice which is which. The difference is in motive. I can say that I want to reach millions of people with the Word of God; this can be both a vision and an ambition. The deciding factor will be why I want to do that. Is it because I want to be famous or is it because I have seen a need for it? One thing I have noticed about God is that whatever area He calls people into, He first shows them a problem or a lack in that area. This is a real vision. For example, when God called Kenneth Hagin into the office of a Prophet, He showed him that His people do not know how He leads them. Therefore, his entire ministry was focused on how the Holy Spirit can lead believers and how to lead a life of faith, which is the life God has called us to lead. If you want to do something and you cannot see a clear need for what you want to do, that may be a sign that you are just ambitious and God is not leading you to do it. Therefore, it is worthwhile going back into the place of prayer and seek the will of God concerning your plans and, most importantly, what He will have you do. This is not just applicable to ministry but to every area of our lives.

Partnership

The Holy Spirit led all of the men mentioned above. Though they may not have known Him as the Holy Spirit at the time, they worked in partnership with Him– submitting to Him as their senior partner. Consider this, how was Abraham able to find the land God called him to and how was he able to recognise the land when he got to it? By the leading of the Holy Spirit, because He is the One that searches out all things and leads us into all truth (**JOHN 16:13, 1 CORINTHIANS 2:10**). The sad thing is that most Christians do not allow the Holy Spirit to lead them and as a result, they cheat themselves of what God has for them. Many ministers have launched out without being filled with the Holy Spirit and are shocked at the result they see.

An example was **David Youngie Cho**. When he started his ministry, he was not yet filled with the Holy Spirit and was only reteaching the sermons of Billie Graham. This strategy worked for him for a while, but it did not take long for him to realise that he was operating on empty. He sought the Lord about this, submitted to the Lordship of the Holy Spirit and watched how his ministry was transformed.

Sadly, many Christians and even Church Leaders have been confronted with the same reality David Cho was confronted with but chose to continue without the Holy Spirit. Even sadder, are those who started with the Holy Spirit but neglected Him along the way because of personal ambition and a lack of personal discipline.

People like Alexander Dowie, Jack Coe, and William Burham are examples of this:

Alexander Dowie – was the first to have a mega Church and was a great Apostle of God but allowed himself to be derailed by people who filled his head with ideologies that were contrary to the will of God. He even considered himself the reincarnation of Elijah and established his city called Zion in the state of Chicago.

Jack Coe – was an extraordinary Evangelist. God used him to heal many people and to provide shelter for orphans as he too was one. However, his boisterous nature – which was spurred by an overly competitive approach towards other ministers and a complacent attitude towards money and his health - led to a devastating and early end of his ministry. God even sent a Kenneth Hagin to warn him about the impending disaster if he did not deal with these three areas of his life, but he did not listen.

William Burham – operated in the gift of the word of knowledge and healing like no one else. The presence of the Holy Spirit was so powerful in his life that he was even able to read the thoughts of others and tell them detailed information about them, including their address and so on. However, when the likes of T L Osbourne and Oral Roberts came on the scene, both of whom operated in the gift of healing and were wonderful orators of the word of God, William Burham became jealous and started teaching as well, even though God had only called him to the ministry of healing. As a result of this, he began to teach strange doctrines and misled many people.

The result for these ministers was:

- Alexander Dowie became a forgotten general of God's army

- Jack Coe and William Burham both died a very tragic and early death. Jack Coe died at age 33 and William Burham at 58.

The prophet **Kenneth Hagin** almost made this mistake when he prioritised his teaching ministry over his prophetic ministry. The

Lord Jesus appeared to him and warned him that if he had continued that way, he would have died at the age of 56. He repented and lived on to age 86. So, thirty years of his life would have been lost because of neglecting the leading of the Holy Spirit.

These examples prove that neglecting the partnership and Lordship of the Holy Spirit can and in so many cases, will lead to an early death, because God will rather take you out of the scene than for you to mislead His people. This is why I believe that in this era of revival we are entering, God will kill a lot of Church leaders, because they are misleading His people. The question to you is will you be one of them? Perhaps it is time to repent.

Those who did not start with the Holy Spirit are already dead even though they are alive. They are only existing but have not started living, and they are at risk of spiritual attacks.

The Church needs to understand that most of the areas we operate in are under the influence of Satanic Principalities, which is why we face persecution and restriction to limit our impact on our environment. Think about it, how many Churches are fighting to keep their place of worship or even struggling to get a place of worship? Why do you think these things are happening? The Principality in that region is putting up a fight:

"For we do not wrestle against flesh and blood, but against principalities, against powers, against the rulers of the darkness of this age, against spiritual hosts of wickedness in the heavenly places." (EPHESIANS 6:12 NKJV)

David Youngie Cho faced this fight when he started his Church in Seoul South Korea. The attendance at his meetings was very low, and he became perplexed because he felt his efforts were in vain. Until one day, he sought the Lord in prayer and that night he had a dream in which he wrestled a woman who had the body of a serpent. In that dream, he cut her head. The following day, his meeting was full. What happened? Jesus said:

"No one can enter a strong man's house and plunder his goods unless he first binds the strong man. And then he will plunder his house." **(MARK 3:27 NKJV)**

The woman or beast that appeared to David Cho was the strong man of the region, the Principality in charge. It was not possible for David Cho's ministry to take off with the Principality still in charge; it needed to be bound before the region could be plundered for God. This is the mistake the Church is making - we have forgotten that everywhere we go is under the control of a Principality. When persecution comes, we begin to wonder why and, to make the matter even worse, we resort to human logic to deal with these issues that we face. In case you missed it the first time, see it again – ***we are not fighting against flesh and blood. We are wrestling against principalities and powers and all the cohorts of Satan.*** Therefore, resorting to human means will never resolve the issue. It is a spiritual battle. This is why Paul started by saying:

"Finally, my brethren, be strong in the Lord and in the power of His might." **(EPHESIANS 6:10 NKJV)**

Who is the power of God's might? The Holy Spirit. This was the power Jesus was talking about when He asked the disciples to wait in Jerusalem until they had received Him. This is because Jesus knew that we could not stand against the wiles of the enemy, we could not bind the strong man and Principality of the regions we go into except by the Holy Spirit. This is why it is impossible to lead a purposeful life unless we are led and are in partnership with the Holy Spirit. The first two points mentioned – though very important – will become irrelevant, wasted or even impossible if we are not in partnership with the Holy Spirit. Our service and vision will be wasted if we do not submit to the Holy Spirit. In fact, it would probably be impossible to serve consistently and be focused on the vision if we are not first submitted to the Holy Spirit. This is perhaps the reason why the qualifying factor to become an ***uihos* of God** is to be led by the Holy Spirit.

It is Time to Manifest

Many Christians are excited at the idea of manifesting the glory of God and be used by God mightily. They want to be part of the revival coming to the Church and are so excited for the spectacular. But sadly, their motives are only to become famous; they want to be MVPs. These are the ***nepios*** we discussed in Chapter 6. However, God is looking for SVPs; people who will serve, be visionaries and most importantly, partner with the Holy Spirit. These are the ***uihos* of God**, called to take their place and manifest the wonders of God in this coming revival. It is time for the ***uihos* of God** to stand up and be counted.

Chapter 8
Stand Up and Take Charge

I thought this book ended at Chapter 7 until I heard a sermon from Pastor Steve Furtick. The sermon was part of the Savage Jesus series, titled, *"You Must be Important."* In the sermon, he recounted the story of how Jesus and his disciples got caught in a storm on their way to the country of the Gadarenes. So why was Jesus on His way there? Perhaps it may be that one of the days he woke up early to pray he heard the demon-possessed man – who terrorised the Gadarenes region – cry out for help and thus set sail to meet him. Therefore, Jesus set sail on purpose; He was on a mission to bring deliverance to a troubled man and to set a region free from the torment of demons. But the enemy stirred up a storm to stop Jesus from reaching the region and setting them free.

Like Jesus, every Christian is called by God, and there are certain things around us that God wants us to take care of, just as Jesus took care of those around him. But do not be surprised that when you stand up to do what God has a laid on your heart to do, a storm will be stirred up to stop you from doing so:

On the same day, when evening had come, He said to them, "Let us cross over to the other side." Now when they had left the multitude, they took Him along in the boat as He was. And other little boats were also with Him. And a great windstorm arose, and the waves beat into the boat, so that it was already filling. But He was in the stern, asleep on a pillow. And they awoke Him and said to Him, "Teacher, do You not care that we are perishing?" (MARK 4: 35 – 38 NKJV)

A closer look at the scripture will show that the storm was intended stop them and to kill them. They were about sink! They were so worried that they resorted to accusing Jesus for not caring. In the same vein, we face storms that were intended to stop us, sap the light out of us and kill us. These storms can appear in several forms – both spiritually and physically, they are a strong resistance from the pits of Hell to stop us from doing God's work and, if we are not careful, they will. But let us see how Jesus handled the storm that the enemy stirred up to resist Him:

Then He arose and rebuked the wind, and said to the sea, "Peace, be still!" And the wind ceased and there was a great calm. But He said to them, "Why are you so fearful? How is it that you have no faith?" And they feared exceedingly, and said to one another, "Who can this be, that even the wind and the sea obey Him!" (Mark 4: 39 – 41 NKJV)

Jesus rebuked the storm and quietened the sea. Then He reprimanded His disciples for not having enough faith. Personally, I thought that was a weird thing to do. How can He reprimand them for fearing for their lives in the wake of a storm, a storm that was about to sink their boat? How can He be upset with them? They should be upset with Him for staying asleep during the storm. Two things will help us explain why Jesus reprimanded His disciples:

1. Jesus said, **"Let us cross over to the other side."**

2. Jesus rose up and rebuked the wind

Stay focused and trust what you heard

Before the storm, we see Jesus telling His disciples that they were going to the other side. As we discussed in Chapter 5 that Jesus was submitted to the leading of the Holy Spirit, therefore, if He said that they were going to the other side, it meant God said they were going to the other side. To be afraid of the storm is to put the reality of the storm above the validity of His Word. When we put anything above the authority of God's Word, we have committed high treason. This was the same thing that Adam and Eve did; they put the fear that God was holding out on them above the authority of His Word.

I had a similar experience when God revealed to me the woman I am to be married to – to whom I gladly am now. But when God showed her to me, I was shocked at the reaction I got from her when I approached to tell her what was on my heart. She was not interested, and to make it worse; she was in a committed relationship. I was heartbroken. Not just because I felt rejected, but also because I thought it would be easy since I had heard from God. How wrong I was. To top it off, many people who were close to me challenged what I heard from God and I began to doubt, continually seeking for confirmation from God, because the reality was not matching up to what God told me and at a point, I almost gave up and considered pursuing someone else I was interested in. However, God saved me from this fatal mistake by reprimanding me, just as He did His disciples and instructed me to go back to the lady He revealed to me in the first instance. My obedience to this instruction set us on course to the bliss of marriage that we are in today.

God wants us to focus on what He said to us in the beginning and trust His Word, even though it may differ from our reality. If we do not trust God in the midst of our storm, we will allow the storm to push us outside the will of God, and as a consequence, we begin to produce Ishmaels.

So, whenever you get caught in a storm, remember what God told you and focus on it.

Take Charge

As I listened to the sermon by Pastor Furtick, I remembered a statement Pastor Christ Oyakhelome made in his sermon, *"The Authority of a Believer"*:

> **"God does not mind bad things happening to you; He does not mind good things happening to you either. What God wants is for you to happen."**

At the time when I was listening to this sermon, I had just proposed to my girlfriend – who is now my wife and shortly after, I was on the brink of being homeless because the business deals I had hoped would pay for my rent collapsed at the last minute. This experience was very devastating. There were some days when I stayed up all night praying that God would enable my business pursuit to succeed so I could pay my rent, but these prayers went unanswered. So, I began to wonder, will God allow me to be homeless or is it His will for this to happen? Once again, I began to doubt, and my heart was broken. Then I heard the sermon where the statement was made:

> **"God does not mind bad things happening to you; He does not mind good things happening to you either. What God wants is for you to happen."**

This statement was not helpful at the time, but reflecting on it now, in the context of this book and Steve Furtick's sermon, I can see why it was important, and it was what I needed. I could also see why prayers are sometimes not answered.

In Chapter 1, we discussed how the fallen angels destroyed the world and how, ever since Adam became enslaved to Satan, the world was subject to the rule of the Satanic hierarchy: Principalities, Powers, Rulers of this Age and Spiritual Wickedness in High Places.

In Chapter 2, we discussed how each nation has a Principality ruling over them and the role of Satanic Principalities and Powers are to ensure that the will of God was not done in that region. I believe that this was what happened when Jesus and His disciples were caught in the storm and when all my businesses failed and I could not pay my rent. The Principalities and Powers stood to resist the will of God from being carried out. Jesus responded to this resistance by rebuking the wind. Therefore, He took charge of the situation. This is the same thing God wants us to do when we face challenges, **Take Charge!**

I will be discussing this area in greater detail in my next book, ***"The Spirit of Prayer and Intercession – The Believers Authority on the Earth"****, which will be a sequel to this book.*

When I reflected on the stories of the people God used, I discovered that God did not make something happen to them, but He helped them happen. For example:

- **Joseph** became governor of Egypt because he interpreted the dreams of Pharaoh and provided counsel that would solve the imminent disaster

- **Moses** brought the plagues on Egypt and divided the Red Sea

- **David** killed Goliath

- **Daniel** proved that it was more profitable to obey God then the king and he became a very prominent man in the land that was designed to enslave him

To better understand what you **'happening'** means, let us consider the example of Moses at the Red Sea:

And the Lord SAID TO MOSES, "Why do you cry to Me? Tell the children of Israel to go forward. But lift up your rod, and stretch out your hand over the sea and divide it. And the children of Israel shall go on dry ground through the midst of the sea. And I indeed will harden the hearts of the Egyptians, and they shall follow them. So I will gain honor over Pharaoh and over all his army, his chariots, and his horsemen. Then the Egyptians shall know that I am the Lord, when I have gained honor for Myself over Pharaoh, his chariots, and his horsemen." (EXODUS 14: 15 – 18 NKJV)

The first statement in this scripture is God reprimanding Moses for praying. God was saying to him, **"Stop asking Me to do something, I have given you the power, so you do it."** This is why some of our prayers are not answered, because we are expecting something to happen to us, but God wants us to happen. I was expecting something to happen to change my circumstance, but God wanted me to happen to my circumstance. This is what the scripture means when it says:

Until the Spirit is poured upon us from on high, And the wilderness becomes a fruitful field, And the fruitful field is counted as a forest. (ISAIAH 32:15 NKJV)

Therefore, it is not God Who will change our circumstances, but we will by the power of the Holy Spirit. This was what Jesus was expecting His disciples to do. However, in order for us to happen, we need to submit to the Lordship of the Holy Spirit and trust in God's Word regardless of the storm.

So, stand up and take charge!

Chapter 9
Rewards and Judgments

The idea to write this Chapter came when my wife showed me a video about a lady who God took to Hell. In that video, she mentioned that she was standing in front of the judgment seat of God and God told her that because she had lived an unappreciated life, He will not send her to Heaven or Hell, but to a place where she will not have access to the presence of God. The statement the lady made reminded me of Rick Joyner's vision of Heaven as recorded in his book, *"Final Quest."* In this book, he recorded how God allowed him to discuss with some of the saints in the Outer Darkness, which included someone who he was supposed to disciple him but did not because of insecurity and a famous reformer who allowed his wife to rule his life.

Jesus spoke about this place in the Parable of Talents:

"Then he who had received the one talent came and said, 'Lord, I knew you to be a hard man, reaping where you have not sown, and gathering where you have not scattered seed. And I was afraid, and went and hid your talent in the ground. Look, there you have *what is yours.'*

"But his lord answered and said to him, 'You wicked and lazy servant, you knew that I reap where I have not sown, and gather where I have not scattered seed. So you ought to have deposited my money with the bankers, and at my coming, I would have received back my own with interest. Therefore take the talent from him, and give it to him who has ten talents.

'For to everyone who has, more will be given, and he will have abundance; but from him who does not have, even what he has

will be taken away. And cast the unprofitable servant into the outer darkness. There will be weeping and gnashing of teeth.' (MATTHEW 25: 24 – 30 NKJV)

The Parable shows us three characters, one who was given five talents and produced ten talents, the second was given two and produced four, the last was given one and went to bury it until Jesus came. On His arrival, Jesus rebuked the servant who hid his talent, took away the talent and sent him into the outer darkness, which was described as a place of weeping and gnashing of teeth. The description of this place has made many believe that this is a type of Hell because weeping and gnashing of teeth signifies agony, pain, and sorrow, which is a fate the souls who are sent to Hell will face. However, it is impossible for this place to be Hell because all the three characters portrayed in the Parable were prototypes of Christians. I say this because Jesus was described as their Lord. This, therefore, are people who have submitted to Lordship of Jesus Christ. If you take a closer look at the character of the one who hid his talent, you will see that it was not an act of defiance against the Lordship of Jesus Christ, but an act of unbelief. Thus, he did not forsake the Lordship of Jesus, which is the only reason a Christian can be sent to Hell.

So, where is the Outer Darkness? In *"Final Quest,"* Rick Joyner described this place as the outmost part of Heaven. Though the presence of God was there, those who were there did not have access to it. It is a place of deep regret and therefore, a place of darkness and torment. It is the same place God was sending the young lady who had the vision of Hell.

A closer look at the scripture shows that the Outer Darkness is a place where those who do not rise to the calling of God on their lives or miss used the gifts that God has given them as a result of selfish ambition and pride. These are the people that Paul spoke about in his letter to the Church at Corinth:

Now if anyone builds on this foundation with gold, silver, precious stones, wood, hay, straw, each one's work will become clear; for the Day will declare it, because it will be revealed by fire; and the fire will test each one's work, of what sort it is. If anyone's work which he has built on it endures, he will receive a reward. If anyone's work is burned, he will suffer loss; but he himself will be saved, yet so as through fire. (1 CORINTHIANS 3: 12 – 15 NKJV)

This scripture shows the judgment every Christian will face when we report back to God at the end of our lives. At this point, everything we have done will be tested by the fire of God. If the works we have done indeed gave glory to God, they will endure, but they did not, they will be consumed with fire, and those whose works are destroyed will be cast into the Outer Darkness.

It is for this reason I have written this book. If we as the Council of gods do not rise and take our place and bring the blessing of God on the Earth, our works will be burnt, and most of us will be cast into the Outer Darkness, just as the wicked servant was.

Apart from the Outer Darkness, there are different levels in Heaven. There are those who will be standing and those who will be sitting on thrones, and more so, there are those whose thrones will be closer to the throne of Jesus. In Rick Joyner's vision, he saw some of the saints in the Bible sitting on thrones. Some of them, such as the Apostle Paul told him that his throne could have been closer to Jesus, if not for some of the mistakes he made by not being sensitive to the Holy Spirit at certain parts of his ministry on the Earth.

Going to Heaven is excellent and very important. Hell is not a place to consider at all. The lady who had the vision of Hell was shown the vision because she was so horrified by the Outer Darkness and asked to be sent to Hell instead. Then God decided to show her what Hell looked like. Hell is real, and it is horrible. It is possible for a Christian to be sent to Hell if they forsake the Lordship of Jesus Christ. However, Hell is not just a place, it is also a mindset, and therefore, it is possible to experience Hell on Earth, we do not allow ourselves to be appropriately disciplined by the Holy Spirit. Hell is also a person and I believe is part of the Spiritual Wickedness in High Places. The Bible says that Hell and Death will be cast into the Lake of Fire. So, Hell is not the final place of the damned, but the Lake of Fire is. It is a place more horrible than anyone can ever imagine. Even Satan and all his cohorts will experience in share agony and be consumed by the fire for all eternity.

Although Hell is not to be considered, just going to Heaven is not enough, we must determine the part of Heaven we go to, whether we will be sitting or standing and how close our throne will be to Jesus. We can do this, by standing up and taking our place as the **uihothesia**. If we do not take our place and exercise the righteousness of God as described in **PSALMS 82**, we will be labelled as the wicked servant and will be cast into the Outer Darkness, a place of eternal regret and torment.

Chapter 10
The Principle of the Chosen

One of the most popular and timeless statements of Jesus Christ is many are called, but few are chosen. This statement, though very clear in its meaning, have led to many questions, such as what is the difference between being called and being chosen and what differentiates the called from the chosen?

These are questions that I had grappled with, also, until recently when I studied the story of Gideon's conquest over the Midianites and the Amalekites. The following will help answer these questions:

Caring for God's People

"Gideon said to Him, "O my lord, if the LORD is with us, why then has all this happened to us? And where are all His miracles which our fathers told us about, saying, 'Did not the LORD bring us up from Egypt?' But now the LORD has forsaken us and delivered us into the hands of the Midianites.'" (JUDGES 6:13 NKJV)

When God appeared to Gideon, the passage above was the response he gave to God's laud description of him. His response demonstrates that Gideon shared in the frustration of the people of Israel. In fact, the scripture showed that he was threading wheat in a winepress to protect his crop from the raiding of the Amalekites and Midianites. He was deeply moved by what was going on that it encouraged him to challenge God about it.

Many people are unhappy about the injustice or immorality they see around them. Some may even discuss it with friends as a recreational activity, but very few people care enough to take the first step in challenging the things that upset them.

One of the principles of the chosen is that they are willing to act on the things that trouble them about their environment. Phinehas is an example of someone who stood out in his time because he acted on what troubled him for the sake of the Children of Israel. He demonstrated this when he killed a fellow Hebrew who was openly whoring with a Midian woman. This singular act ended the disaster that God sent within the Israelite camp, and God made a covenant of peace and everlasting priesthood to him and his generation **(NUMBERS 25: 6 – 12)**. David was another example of someone who acted on what troubled him for the sake of the people of Israel. He was troubled by the taunting of Goliath and the disrepute that it brought on the name of the Lord, that he risked his life by going out to fight against Goliath and defeated him. A feat that none of the valiant soldiers were willing to do, not even the king Saul **(1 SAMUEL 17)**.

Just like Gideon, Phinehas, and David, many have ideas on how to solve the problems around them. These ideas are God calling us, but our decision to rise to the occasion is what makes us chosen.

Know your weakness and limitations

"So he said to Him, "O my Lord, how can I save Israel? Indeed my clan is the weakest in Manasseh, and I am the least in my father's house."' **(JUDGES 6:15 NKJV)**

Gideon was conscious of his reality. This may seem contradictory to the concept of faith, especially from a Pente-charismatic perspective, but true faith can only come when we accept our weaknesses and inadequacies. Paul came to an understanding of this truth when he mentioned that he glories in his weaknesses so the power of Christ will rest upon him **(2 CORINTHIANS 12:10)**. This realisation Paul had shows that we can only experience the power of God when we are aware and embrace our weaknesses, trusting alone in His power to be manifested in us.

Further to the above, if we look at the story of Samuel anointing David, we will see that Eliab appeared to be more fitting to be a king than David. In fact, Samuel was about to anoint him, until he was interrupted by God. Eliab represents those who are confident in their abilities to do the work God has called them to do. These people will always be surprised when God rejects them because they have only trusted in themselves alone.

Honour the presence of God

"Then he said to Him, "If now I have found favor in Your sight, then show me a sign that it is You who talk with me. Do not depart from here, I pray until I come to You and bring out my offering and set it before You."' (JUDGES 6: 17 – 18 NKJV)

After confessing his inadequacies to God, the next thing we see Gideon do is to honour the presence of God by giving Him an offering. A similar example of honouring the presence of God through a heartfelt offering is seen right from the beginning of time when Abel gave God his first fruits and his offering was chosen ahead of Cain's, his brother. We see this same principle at play when Solomon gave a great offering to God and consequently, God appeared to him and made him one of the most influential kings to walk the face of the Earth.

However, it is also critical to understand that honouring God is not about giving material offerings alone, but it more about the response of heart towards God. I say this because God owns cattle on a thousand hills, if He is hungry, He will not tell us, because He is the one that feeds us in the first place and the offering we give to Him can only at best be a sacrificial token out of what He has provided for us. Therefore, God is not moved by what we offer, but with the heart with which we offer it.

It is also essential for us to note that though we may already be chosen, the moment we begin to dishonour the presence of God, we are at risk of being deselected and even deleted from the mandate given to us by God. This was the fate Moses suffered when he disregarded the command of God to speak to the rock, instead, driven by frustration from the people, he struck the rock twice and was disqualified from entering the Promised Land.

Be willing to do the Unpopular

"And when the men of the city arose early in the morning, there was the altar of Baal, torn down; and the wooden image that was beside it was cut down, and the second bull was being offered on the altar which had been built. So they said to one another, "Who has done this thing?" And when they had inquired and asked, they said, "Gideon the son of Joash has done this thing."' (JUDGES 6: 28 – 29 NKJV)

For us to be chosen by God, we must be willing to do what others see as unpopular. This is a fundamental criterion by which God uses to select the men and women He has used throughout history. If we cannot break through the mould of the fear of what others will think about us, God cannot use us. This was a lesson God needed to teach Gideon. For God to use Him, he first had to destroy the altar his father had built to Baal, which resulted in the people in that region wanting to kill him.

Obedience to God may sometimes mean going against the belief system of those you love and respect most. However, if you want to be used by God at all, you will need to be ready to go against the opinion of others, regardless of what the consequence may be. History is full of people who came to death because of their devotion to God. Jesus Christ was part of those people, and we know that through His death and resurrection, we have a place with God forever. Therefore, we can be assured that even if our devotion leads to death, we will yet be alive forever in Christ, in God. This is indeed a glorious heritage we have, the opportunity to live and die for the One Who did the same for us. Those who are willing to do this will reign with Him in this age and in the age to come.

Do not trust in numbers

"But the LORD *said to Gideon, "The people* are *still* too *many; bring them down to the water, and I will test them for you there. Then it will be,* that *of whom I say to you, 'This one shall go with you,' the same shall go with you; and of whomever I say to you, 'This one shall not go with you,' the same shall not go."* (JUDGES 7:4 NKJV)

It is easy to be confident when you have many people on your side. However, one thing about human nature is that allegiance and loyalty is very fickle and can consequently change at any time. Therefore, if our confidence is in numbers, then we have an insecure confidence. It is, for this reason, I believe God told Gideon that the people in his company were too much for Him to use to deliver Israel from the bondage of Midian. God wanted to show Gideon that victory is not in numbers, but the power of God.

The test of rest

So he brought the people down to the water. And the LORD *said to Gideon, "Everyone who laps from the water with his tongue, as a dog laps, you shall set apart by himself; likewise everyone who gets down on his knees to drink." And the number of those who lapped,* putting *their hand to their mouth, was three hundred men; but all the rest of the people got down on their knees to drink water. Then the* LORD *said to Gideon, "By the three hundred men who lapped I will save you, and deliver the Midianites into your hand. Let all the* other *people go, every man to his place."'* (JUDGES 7: 5 – 7 NKJV)

Do you know that it is easier to be faithful to God in times of trouble than in times of rest? This is a paradoxical reality that many of God's people fall victim for. A perfect example of this notion is Asa. When the Ethiopians came against Judah with one million soldiers, Asa trusted in God with six hundred thousand soldiers to defeat the Ethiopians, and he did. However, when Israel (a nation smaller than Ethiopia) came against Judah, he no longer relied on God but sought the help of Syria – a heathen nation – to deliver him from the power of his enemies. He did not know that he was reaching out to a nation that God intended to bring under the control of his kingdom (**2 Chronicles 16**).

The story of Asa raises the question of trusting God in the place of rest. When everything seems to be going well, will we still trust God for direction and instruction or would we rely on our own means. This is the test of rest that God used to try the men in Gideon's company. The water represents the place of rest and how they refreshed themselves was an indication of where their heart was and who they relied on.

Those who put their hand to mouth are the ones who got lost in the place of rest and consequently, let their guard down and trusted more in the water than in God. These ones are like Asa who trusted in Syria more than the power of God. Therefore, they were deselected and left behind.

The group that lapped with their tongue represent those who stayed alert even in the place of rest. They did not deny themselves of the rest, but their eyes kept scanning for danger and always trusting in God for what to do next.

Staying sensitive

"'It happened on the same night that the LORD *said to him, "Arise, go down against the camp, for I have delivered it into your hand. But if you are afraid to go down, go down to the camp with Purah your servant, and you shall hear what they say; and afterward your hands shall be strengthened to go down against the camp."'* (JUDGES 7: 9 – 11 NKJV)

One of the mistakes we make as God's people is that when God gives us one instruction, we close our ears to the others to come and when we get into trouble, we begin to question whether we had heard from God. We seem to forget that God speaks in stages, just as the GPRS system does.

Imagine if, when you put on your Satnav, and it says turn left, after which you switch it off and keep turning left at each junction. Will you get to the intended destination? Most probably not, in fact, you are bound to get lost. In the same vein when God instructs us to do something, setting out to do it is excellent, but we need to keep listening for further instructions, so we know what He will have us do at each junction.

Looking at the scriptural reference above, if Gideon had not obeyed God by going to the camp of the enemy, it would not have mattered that he destroyed the altar his father built to Baal. It would not have mattered that he took only 300 men as God commanded, he would have still failed because he did not stay sensitive to God's leading. Sadly, many of God's people, who were indeed called and chosen by God, have failed because of this. If we do not stay sensitive to God, it would have been better if we did not answer the call in the first instance, because we will fail and our fate may be worse than at the beginning. Worst of all, we would have misled many by our disobedience, leading them to destruction. Therefore, it is vital that we stay sensitive to the leading of the Holy Spirit.

Stay humble

"'Then the men of Israel said to Gideon, "Rule over us, both you and your son, and your grandson also; for you have delivered us from the hand of Midian." But Gideon said to them, "I will not rule over you, nor shall my son rule over you; the LORD *shall rule over you."'* (JUDGES 8: 22 – 23 NKJV)

Humility is hard to maintain when we are victorious, but it is what is needed for us to stay victorious. After Gideon had defeated the Midianites, the people wanted him to be their ruler, but instead, Gideon said, *"The* LORD *shall rule over you."* This statement is very powerful because Gideon did not allow his conquest to ascribe to him what God did not give him. This is a very big lesson to the Church, especially to those that God will use in this season because we cannot ascribe to ourselves what was not given to us because of what we have achieved, or better still, what God has done through us.

Many people have fallen into this delusion, and as a result, we have put ourselves in places that were only reserved for God.

In a vision given to me by God in 2010, I was told that I am called to be a general in God's army, but there is only One Captain, Jesus. In the same vein, God has called us to be gods on the Earth, but this does not in any way mean that we are God; it only means that we are representing Him here on the Earth and as a result, we are accountable to Him. We are not gods to be worshipped, but we are gods sent to serve. Jesus alone is the head of the Church, and only He will rule His people, we are merely tools in the hands of the Holy Spirit.

Epilogue
A Message to the Church

I would like to end this book as I started. **I can hear the sound of the abundance of rain**. However, the rain is not necessarily the manifestation of the spectacular, but a call to purpose.

As the theme scripture of this book says:

"God stands in the congregation of the mighty; He judges among the gods. How long will you judge unjustly, and show partiality to the wicked? Defend the poor and fatherless; do justice to the afflicted and needy. Deliver the poor and needy; free them from the hand of the wicked. They do not know, nor do they understand; they walk about in darkness; all the foundations of the earth are unstable. I said, "You are gods, and all of you are children of the Most High. But you shall die like men, and fall like one of the princes." (PSALM 82: 1 – 7 NKJV)

This scripture gives us a full picture of what God is saying to the Church. God is standing in the Council of gods. As we have established in this book, we are the gods being described in this passage. But God is questioning us. He is challenging us. He is calling us back to purpose and reminding us of our identity and role.

This chastisement shows that it is our job as the Church to keep the Earth from returning to the state of chaos it was in **GENESIS 1:2**. It is our job to redeem the desolate heritages and deliver them from the habitations of cruelty. It is the job of the Church to be the voice of the oppressed, the afflicted, the broken-hearted, the downtrodden and to deliver the poor and the needy. We are the solution the world is seeking, but they are angry with us and even persecute us because we are not standing up to be counted. So, God asks again:

"How long? How long shall the oppressor go without justice and the poor without food? How long will the world be covered in darkness and cruelty remain the order of the day? Again, how long? For I have said, you are gods, My children – children of the Most High. But how long will it take for you to take your place and be the light that you are to the world I have created?"

Our Father is calling us; He is looking for His champions – His **uihos**. This message is not just to the Church as a whole, but to every Christian. **Will you be an SVP?** Will you stand and be counted as the heroes of the Old Testament were? This is the revival that is coming to the Earth:

"For many waves of revival have come on the Earth," says the Lord, "But none of these will compare to what I am sending now. For indeed, the latter rain shall be greater than the former. This shall not just be a revival of meetings, but a revival of healing and the restoration of that which was lost. Not just the healing of body and soul, but the healing of nations", says the Lord, "A restoring of order and the dispelling of cruelty and desolation, as my uihos rise and take their place, bringing My will upon the Earth. This shall happen speedily and the time is now!" so says the living God.

I am not sure I have done justice to this message. I hope that the little message communicated will be a catalyst that will create a change in the body of Christ. It is time for the Church and every Christian to stand up and be counted. We can no longer be **nepios**, but it is time to come into **uihothesia.** To become luminaries – lights and standard of moral excellence, and shine for God. We are called to be **THE SONS OF GOD**.

God bless you,
Tolulope Oyewole

Notice

Tolulope Oyewole is available to hold speaking engagements, seminars and workshops at your church or fellowship regarding the topics discussed in this book and other Christian related topics. For more information, please contact us on info@toministries.org *or visit our website:* www.toministries.org *for more information.*

We hope to connect with you.

"A bad relationship has the power to bring out the worst in you. Be careful who you choose to relate with."